WE'RE NUMBER ONE!

WE'RE NUMBER ONE!

WHERE AMERICA STANDS—AND FALLS— IN THE NEW WORLD ORDER

ANDREW L. SHAPIRO

VINTAGE BOOKS

A DIVISION OF RANDOM HOUSE, INC.

NEW YORK

A Vintage Original, May 1992
First Edition

Copyright © 1992 by Andrew L. Shapiro

All rights reserved under International and Pan-American
Copyright Conventions. Published in the United States by Vintage Books,
a division of Random House, Inc., New York, and simultaneously
in Canada by Random House of Canada Limited, Toronto.

Library of Congress Cataloging-in-Publication Data
Shapiro, Andrew L.
We're number one!: where America stands—and falls—in the new
world order / Andrew L. Shapiro.
p. cm.
"A Vintage original."
ISBN 0-679-73893-2
1. United States—Economic conditions—1981–   2. United States—
Social conditions—1980–   3. Economic history—1990–
4. Competition, International.   I. Title.
HC106.8.S47   1992
317.3—dc20   91-58069
CIP

Pages 203–204 constitute an extension of this copyright page.

Manufactured in the United States of America
10 9 8 7 6 5 4 3 2 1

For my parents, Daniel and Ellen Shapiro

"All for number one"

—James Joyce

"We are Number One . . . and we're going to stay that way."
—President George Bush

ACKNOWLEDGMENTS

Many people contributed to the creation of this book, but three individuals were truly indispensable: Joe Spieler, my agent, who was (and is) the man with the vision; Marty Asher, my editor, who molded a book out of a blur of ideas and statistics; and Joi Anderson, my research assistant, confidante, and coconspirator from beginning to end. Special thanks go to Victor Navasky and the staff of *The Nation* (which published the piece that launched this book); to those generous souls who read drafts and made suggestions; to my students and colleagues at The Dalton School; and to all the family members, mentors, friends, and strangers who listened to my ideas. You're Number One!

CONTENTS

INTRODUCTION

In the year following our victory in the Persian Gulf and the collapse of communism, the "We're Number One!" ethos has been born again in America. President George Bush assures us we are the "undisputed leader of the world." "Still No. 1," says *The New York Times*. First in overall standard of living, trumpets *Money* magazine.[1] Even ascendant Germany and Japan seem to have been eclipsed.

But as our economy remains sluggish, as health care becomes a critical issue in our nation, and as faith in government and politicians falls lower and lower, the American people want to know: Is the United States *really* Number One?

Well, the truth is we *are* Number One, but not the way the politicians and experts would have us think.

America is, for example, Number One in billionaires—and we're Number One in children living in poverty among the nineteen major industrial nations. We're Number One in health care spending and we're Number One in infant mortality. We're Number One in belief in God and we're Number One in murder. Paradoxes of American life like these form the narrative of this book, shedding new light on what it means to be Number One.

Unlike other analyses of the United States' position in an increasingly competitive world, this book exposes *all* areas of American achievement. The United States is wealthy and poor, medically advanced and chronically ill, highly educated and highly uninformed. What we say is often at odds with what we do. For example, we're Number One in percentage of students who say they are good at math and last in percentage of students who *are* good at math. In short, this book shows where America really stands—and falls—in international comparisons of health care, education, the economy, life-style, politics, crime, the environment, media, and other vital areas.

We're Number One! began as a response to the Persian Gulf war. As our troops returned from the Middle East, America was infused with pride that distracted us, consciously or not, from our domestic malaise. The war induced a collective amnesia in which we temporarily forgot the bad news about our decline relative to the Japanese, the Germans, and other major industrial powers. *We're Number One!* points out the dangers of allowing pride to overshadow reality as the century comes to an end.

Some readers may find this book too critical of America. They may even call it unpatriotic. But I believe that it is only by facing our flaws and weaknesses that we can break out of our complacency, confront our massive problems and surmount them. Ronald Reagan gave us morning in America. Now we need to wake up!

AUTHOR'S NOTE

I approached this project as a curious citizen, not as a statistician. I place more faith in trends than in specific numbers, and while I believe (to a certain degree) that statistics can be found to tell any story, the overwhelming preponderance of evidence from the cited sources is formidable. Figures will change from year to year. We may have slipped from Number One to Number 2 or even Number 8 in some category in the time it took to produce this book. But, there is a narrative in these pages which speaks for itself.

The statistics included here are from the most reliable and recent sources available (international statistics take years to gather and tabulate, so data from the mid and late 1980s are often considered current).[1] The figures come largely from the Organization for Economic Cooperation and Development, and the United Nations and its agencies: the World Bank; International Monetary Fund; World Health Organization; International Labor Organization; United Nations Educational, Scientific and Cultural Organization; United Nations Development Programme; the Food and Agriculture Organization; and others. International opinion data are also taken from the most reliable and recent sources, the largest of which is the World Values Survey (details about the World Values Survey can be found in the endnotes).[2]

All statistics are fully cited in the body of the work or in the notes at the end of the book. Dates used in charts (e.g. 1985–

1991) reflect the most recent years for which data are available. Due to space constraints, some of the more arcane findings (We're Number One in Elvis impersonators, pet cemeteries, shoe consumption, etc.) had to be left in my posterity file.

Throughout the book I use the term "the nineteen major industrial nations" to refer to those countries that are most comparable to the United States in social and economic development. Most of the comparisons are made between the United States and the remainder of these nineteen major industrial nations: Australia, Austria, Belgium, Canada, Denmark, Finland, France, Germany, Ireland, Italy, Japan, the Netherlands, New Zealand, Norway, Spain, Sweden, Switzerland, and the United Kingdom. Information on other relevant nations is occasionally included; that explains why we may be Number 25 or even Number 55 in some category or other. But most often comparisons are limited to those of the nineteen major industrial nations for which data on a specific subject is available. References to Germany include data from the former Federal Republic of Germany (West Germany) only, unless otherwise specified. References to the Soviet Union refer to the period before the dissolution of the nation in the latter part of 1991.

WE'RE NUMBER ONE!

CHRONIC DISORDER

HEALTH AND MEDICAL CARE

The American health care system is the most advanced and the most inequitable of the major industrial nations. Though our per capita spending on health and medical care is unparalleled in the world, the United States is the only Western democracy without a national health care plan covering all citizens. Americans are beginning to voice their discontent: two thirds of those polled say they would prefer a nationalized health care system like Canada's.[1]

Health care is sure to be one of the major issues in American elections in 1992 and beyond, and with good reason: from infant mortality to life expectancy, our country's health is poorer than that of Japan, Australia, Canada, and most European nations. This is particularly true for blacks in America, who are twice as likely as whites to say their health is fair or poor, and for our children, who are rightfully called "the most neglected in the developed world."[2]

The frustration produced by America's paradoxical health system is well captured in the following words of one health care expert: "How could a medical system that costs so much have become so inadequate? Why is the infant mortality rate rising? Measles causing disease, even death? More and more middle-class Americans denied health insurance? The AIDS epidemic spreading unchecked in poor, minority communities? The mentally ill hallucinating on our streets? What happened to the best health care system in the world?"[3]

LIFE EXPECTANCY

- **We're Number 15 in life expectancy.**

No indicator is as important as average life expectancy in measuring a nation's health. While this may seem obvious—staying alive is the ultimate objective of health care—the simplicity of this point is sometimes obfuscated by the rush of health statistics now at our disposal.

The Japanese are the healthiest people in the world, judging by average life expectancy; they outlive Americans by nearly three years. Fourteen countries have longer average life expectancies than the United States' 75.9 years. The great discrepancy between developed and developing nations in average life expectancy underscores the lack of health resources available to the world's poorer nations.[4] A quarter century of life separates the average life expectancy of 76.4 years in the most developed nations and 50.7 years in the least developed nations.[5] Sierra Leone and Afghanistan have the lowest life expectancies of any nation: 42 years.

The fact that the world's wealthiest nation, the United States, ranks fifteenth in this category shows the gap in availability of health care within our own country, a gap that runs along racial as well as class lines. The average life expectancy for blacks in America is 71.4 years, five years less than that of whites. For black men, average life expectancy is 67.7 years, lower than the rate in such countries as China, Malaysia, Albania, Mexico, and Uruguay.[6] In Harlem, a black man is less likely to reach age 65 than a man living in Bangladesh, one of the world's poorest nations.[7]

Women in the United States and most developed nations live seven years longer than men on average. The average life expectancy is 79.6 years for white women compared to 72.7 years for white men, and 75.0 years for black women compared to 67.7 years for black men.[8]

Life expectancy at birth in years, 1990:

COUNTRY	LIFE EXPECTANCY	COUNTRY	LIFE EXPECTANCY
Japan	78.6	Italy	76.0
Iceland	77.8	**United States**	**75.9**
Sweden	77.4	Israel	75.9
Switzerland	77.4	Denmark	75.8
Hong Kong	77.3	United Kingdom	75.7
Netherlands	77.2	Finland	75.5
Norway	77.1	Belgium	75.2
Canada	77.0	Germany[9]	75.2
Spain	77.0	New Zealand	75.2
Australia	76.5	Austria	74.8
France	76.4	Ireland	74.6
Cyprus	76.2	**U.S. black**	**71.4**
Greece	76.1	USSR	70.6

Sources: United Nations Development Programme, *Human Development Report 1991* (New York: Oxford University Press, 1991), pp. 122, 174; U.S. black projected figure: U.S. Bureau of the Census, *Statistical Abstract of the United States 1991* (Washington, D.C.: USGPO, 1991), p. 73.

SPENDING AND COVERAGE

- **We're Number One in total health spending.**
- **We're Number 13 in public health spending.**

America spends more on health care than any country in the world, in both per capita terms and as a percentage of gross domestic product. But when private dollars are removed and public expenditures are considered alone, the United States is thirteenth in health care spending among the nineteen major industrial countries. Only Switzerland and Japan spend less in relative terms.

In the average industrial nation, public spending accounts for more than three quarters of all expenditures on health care. In the United States, it accounts for only 40 percent, leaving the majority of the $700 billion spent on health care each year to be paid out of the citizen's pocket.[10] The scope of the private burden in the United States is illustrated by the fact that a larger share of household spending goes toward health care in America than in any other industrial nation for which figures are available.[11]

Does paying more guarantee good health care? "Many Americans comfort themselves with the belief that, even if their system is by far the most costly and least equitable of any in the industrialized democracies, at least it provides 'the world's best care' for those who can afford it," says one publication of the Organization for Economic Cooperation and Development. "But if 'best' is defined in terms of outcomes achieved, rather than as a simple linear function of cost, then the evidence suggests that even this is wishful thinking. 'More' is not the same as 'better.' What America provides is not the world's best, but the world's most, and most highly priced."[12]

Why is health care in America so costly? Primarily because of costs related to the private-sector control of our system: complex billing and open-ended reimbursement for doctors and hospitals; overhead for fifteen hundred private health insurance companies; and employment of insurance agents and other administrative personnel who do not provide direct services.[13] A national health insurance plan, according to one estimate, could cut administrative costs almost in half, from about 22 to 12 percent of all health spending (Canada spends 11 percent on administrative costs), for savings of around $70 billion.[14]

A national health insurance plan might also ease the burden on American businesses, particularly small employers, who have seen a huge increase in the cost of health care for workers. "In the 1960s, businesses spent about 4 to 8 cents of each dollar of profits on health care. In 1990, it was 25 to 50 cents per dollar and rising," writes Philip J. Hilts in *The New York Times*.[15] Still, the percentage of employee health insurance premiums paid by employers dropped from 80 to 69 percent between 1980 and 1989.[16] Perhaps that's why health care coverage was a factor in 78 percent of all labor strikes in 1989, up from just 18 percent in 1986, according to the Service Employees International Union.[17]

European countries with national insurance plans spend less than we do on health care and generally fare better in the standard indicators of life expectancy and infant mortality. In addition to looking abroad for health care models, the U.S. federal government should consider Hawaii, the one state in the union that has provided almost all its inhabitants with health care through a combination of employer and state coverage.[18]

The opinion of the medical industry on the issue of nationalized care is not exactly clear. Fifty-six percent of American doctors say they favor a national health insurance program, but 74 percent believe that most of their colleagues oppose such a program.[19] While the merits of nationalized health care for the United States will continue to be debated by doctors, industry experts, and politicians, the American people unequivocally favor an increase in public health spending.[20]

**Total health expenditure as a percent of gross domestic product
(GDP), and in real dollars per capita, 1990. Public health
expenditure as a percent of GDP, 1990:**

COUNTRY	TOTAL (% OF GDP)	TOTAL PER CAPITA	PUBLIC (% OF GDP)
Sweden	8.7	$1,421	7.8
Norway	7.2	1,281	6.9
Canada	9.0	1,795	6.7
France	8.9	1,379	6.6
Finland	7.4	1,156	6.2
Belgium	7.4	1,087	6.1
Germany	8.1	1,287	5.9
Italy	7.7	1,113	5.9
Netherlands	8.0	1,182	5.9
New Zealand	7.2	853	5.9
Ireland	7.1	697	5.8
Austria	8.4	1,192	5.6
Australia	7.5	1,151	5.2
Denmark	6.2	963	5.2
Spain	6.6	730	5.2
United Kingdom	6.1	909	5.2
United States	**12.4**	**2,566**	**5.2**
Switzerland	7.4	1,389	5.1
Japan	6.5	1,113	4.9
Average	7.8	1,224	5.9

Source: Organization for Economic Cooperation and Development (Paris), Health Data file, 1991.

- **We're Number One in percentage of population
  without health insurance.**

The main reason we're Number One in percentage of population without health insurance is that we're last in percentage of
population covered by *public* health insurance. Only about one
fifth of Americans qualify for the main types of public health
insurance available in the United States: Medicare, Medicaid,
and veterans' benefits.[21]

Of those who don't qualify, many have private insurance.[22]
But almost one in seven Americans (34 million people—most

living in families *with* a working adult) have no insurance at all, and one in four (63 million) have been without insurance for a substantial period of time during the last two years. Many more have inadequate coverage, meaning that they could be bankrupted by a major illness.[23] In fact, one health care expert says that because only 1 percent of the population has private long-term-care insurance, "virtually *any* American could be impoverished by a prolonged disabling illness."[24] Additionally, as many as 40 percent of those eligible for some forms of public aid do not receive it. These gaps in health care result directly from the fact that the United States is the only major industrialized nation (other than South Africa) without a national health insurance plan providing universal coverage while controlling costs.

Percentage of population covered by public health insurance, 1990:[25]

COUNTRY	PERCENT	COUNTRY	PERCENT
Australia	100	Sweden	100
Canada	100	United Kingdom	100
Denmark	100	Austria	99
Finland	100	France	99
Ireland	100	Switzerland	99
Italy	100	Spain	99
Japan	100	Belgium	98
New Zealand	100	Germany	92
Netherlands	100	**United States**	**21**
Norway	100		

Sources: Organization for Economic Cooperation and Development (Paris), Health Data file, 1991; U.S.: National Center for Health Statistics, *Advance Data*, No. 201, June 18, 1991.

- **We're Number One in NOT offering paid maternity leave.**

The inadequacy of America's health care system is apparent in the fact that the United States does not have a national policy guaranteeing paid maternity leave from work for women. Maternity leave is not only good social policy; it is crucial to the health of infant and mother alike. More than seventy of the world's nations have a national maternity leave policy, including Algeria, Botswana, China, Djibouti, Egypt, Fiji, Ghana, and all developed nations—except the United States. Iraq provides women with ten weeks of maternity leave at full pay.[26] Paid maternity leave, ranging from 60 to 100 percent of salary, is also the standard in most of the nineteen major industrial nations. Maternity leave is obligatory in many countries, and paternity leave is an option for Norwegian and German fathers as well. At the time of delivery, Spanish fathers are given three free days off by law.

Why is the United States so far behind on the issue of parental leave? Though almost all American companies offer maternity leave, it is not always paid, and since it is not guaranteed nationwide by law, many women worry justifiably about job security. Responding to the needs of two-parent families, almost one third of American companies now also offer paternity leave, according to a recent survey; but only about 1 percent of eligible men actually take the leave.[27] Again, because this option is not sanctioned by law, many men consider it a job risk to take available paternity leave.

The answer, according to many policymakers, is to give the United States what most countries already have: a national parental leave policy. "The United States," says one state government official, "is the last holdout of the world's industrialized countries against making a formal, national commitment to families."[28] Efforts at the federal level to obtain a parental leave bill have been unsuccessful. A bill passed by Congress in 1990, the Family Leave Act, was vetoed by President Bush. Seven out of ten Americans polled say they favor this type of law.[29]

Duration of nationally provided paid maternity leave in weeks, 1988:

COUNTRY	WEEKS	COUNTRY	WEEKS
United Kingdom	40	Germany	14
Finland	38	Ireland	14
Denmark	28	Japan	14
France	16–28	Spain	14
Italy	22	Netherlands	12
Norway	20	Sweden	12
Canada	17–18	Switzerland	8–12
Austria	16	**United States**	**0**
Belgium	14		

Source: International Labor Organization, "Work and Family: The Child Care Challenge," *Conditions of Work Digest,* vol. 7, February 1988.

CONTRACEPTION, PREGNANCY, AND ABORTION

- **We're Number 11 in use of contraceptives.**
- **We're Number One in abortion.**

Being Number 11 in contraceptive usage may explain why we're Number One in abortions among the nineteen major industrial nations. Seventy-four percent of U.S. women currently use birth control.[30] In at least ten other nations, a larger percentage of women use contraceptives. As a result, American women have the second highest pregnancy rate among the nineteen major industrial nations; only Ireland's rate is higher. The average American woman experiences 2.56 pregnancies in her lifetime. More than two thirds of pregnancies in the United States result in birth; the remainder are terminated by abortion (excluding miscarriages).[31]

Abortion continues to be as explosive an issue as any in our nation, and there is ample fuel for the fire. More than a million and a half abortions were performed in the United States in 1988, the most recent year for which data is available. That makes us Number One among the nineteen major industrial nations in abortions performed per capita and percentage of pregnancies ending in abortion. An American woman is twice as likely to have an abortion as a woman in Canada or Germany, and five times as likely as a woman in Ireland. Our rates are, however, substantially lower than that of the former USSR, Bulgaria, and Romania, where it is not uncommon for 50 percent or more of pregnancies to end in abortion.

The U.S. abortion rate is particularly high among young women, the poor, and minorities. According to the Alan Guttmacher Institute, women under age 25 account for nearly 60 percent of all abortions, poor women are about three times as likely as other women to have an abortion, and the rate of abortion among nonwhite women is nearly three times that of white women (56 vs. 21 per 1,000). Surprisingly, Catholic women are 30 percent more likely to have an abortion than Protestant women.[32]

Percentage of pregnancies ending in abortion (excluding miscarriages), 1986–88; and percentage of married women age 15 to 44 using contraceptives, 1980–88:[33]

COUNTRY[34]	PREGNANCIES ENDING IN ABORTION	CONTRACEPTIVE PREVALENCE
United States	**29.0**	**74**
Denmark	27.0	63
Japan	27.0	56
Italy	25.7	78
Sweden	24.9	78
Norway	22.2	84
Australia	20.4	76
United Kingdom	18.6	81
Finland	18.0	80
France	17.3	80
Switzerland	15.0	71
Canada	14.7	73
New Zealand	13.6	70
Germany	12.1	77
Netherlands	9.0	76
Belgium	8.7	81
Ireland	5.9	—

Sources: Stanley K. Henshaw and Evelyn Morrow, *Induced Abortion: A World Review, 1990 Supplement* (New York: Alan Guttmacher Institute, 1990), p. 12; Alan Guttmacher Institute, *Facts in Brief: Abortion in the United States* (New York: AGI, 1991); Mary Beth Weinberger, "Recent Trends in Contraceptive Use," United Nations Population Division paper presented at Demographic and Health Surveys Conference, Washington, D.C., 1991.

• **We're Number One in abortions obtained by women who have had an abortion before.**

Percentage of women having an abortion who have had at least one before, 1985–87:

COUNTRY	PERCENT	COUNTRY	PERCENT
United States	**40.6**	Canada	22.1
Denmark	38.0	Netherlands	21.6
Sweden	34.7	France	19.0
Italy	30.1	United Kingdom[35]	17.7
Norway	26.8	New Zealand	17.5
Finland	25.6		

Source: Stanley K. Henshaw and Evelyn Morrow, *Induced Abortion: A World Review, 1990 Supplement* (New York: Alan Guttmacher Institute, 1990), p. 22.

- **We're Number One in ignorance of biology.**
- **We're Number One in teen-age pregnancy.**

Teen-age pregnancy is a problem of ignorance as well as negligence (the stork makes the baby, right?). If our young people's performance on a recent international biology test is any indicator of their knowledge of reproduction, we may have an explanation for why we're Number One in teen-age pregnancy. The United States scored last among the thirteen countries where the test was given, including not only Canada and Japan, but Poland, Hungary, Hong Kong, and Singapore. Our students answered 37.9 percent of the questions correctly; Singapore performed the best, with an average of 66.8 percent correct.[36]

One in ten American young women age 15 to 19 (one in five who are sexually active) becomes pregnant each year. This rate, the highest of the nineteen major industrial nations, is not due to an unusual amount of sexual activity among U.S. teen-agers, but rather to inadequate sex education and lack of access to contraceptives. The United States has twice as many teen-age pregnancies per capita as the United Kingdom, three times as many as Sweden, and more than six times as many as the Netherlands, according to a comprehensive international study of teen-age pregnancy sponsored by the Alan Guttmacher Institute. The pregnancy rate for white teen-agers alone is higher than that of all of the nineteen major industrial nations. Pregnancy rates for nonwhite American teen-agers are twice as high as those of whites: 41 percent of white women and 63 percent of nonwhite women have experienced at least one pregnancy by age 20.

America's high rate of teen-age pregnancy is a direct result of low contraceptive use among its youth. The Alan Guttmacher Institute's study of teen-age pregnancy concludes that "the United States could well have the lowest level of use" of contraceptives among teen-agers of any of the countries surveyed.[37] Sixty-five percent of sexually active American adolescent females use a contraceptive when they first have intercourse, and

79 percent use birth control regularly. A greater percentage of teen-age girls use contraceptives in the U.K., Sweden, and Canada than in the United States, where clinics are also less abundant and doctors are less likely to prescribe birth control to an unmarried teen-ager without parental consent.

Half of our teen-age pregnancies result in birth, 36 percent in abortion, and the remainder in miscarriage. Our teen-age birthrate—about one birth per twenty girls—is also the highest of the nineteen major industrial nations. Two thirds of teen-age mothers are not married. Most alarming is the fact that "the maximum difference in birthrates between the U.S. and other countries occurs among the most vulnerable teenagers, girls under 15."[38] Each year, more than ten thousand American girls age 14 and under give birth.

Teen-age mothers are more likely to experience health complications at birth, economic difficulties, and problems finishing their education than are women who have children at a later age. Families begun by teen-age mothers cost the U.S. government $21 billion in health and welfare services in 1989; and the problem is getting worse. The United States is the only developed country where teen-age pregnancy has increased in recent years. During this period, conservative views toward sexuality have regained prominence in America, challenging sex education, the distribution of condoms in public schools, and reproductive rights in general. In contrast, the countries with the lowest teen-age pregnancy rates are, according to the Alan Guttmacher Institute, the ones with "the most liberal attitudes toward sex, the most easily accessible contraceptive services for teenagers and the most effective formal and informal programs for sex education."[39]

Birthrates per 1,000 teen-age women age 15 to 19, the nineteen major industrial nations, 1980–81:

COUNTRY	RATE	COUNTRY	RATE
United States	**53**	France	23
U.S. (white only)	**45**	Ireland	23
New Zealand	39	Italy	23
Austria	35	Germany	20
United Kingdom[40]	29	Finland	19
Australia	28	Denmark	16
Spain	27	Sweden	14
Canada	26	Switzerland	10
Norway	25	Netherlands	9
Belgium	23	Japan	4

Sources (for chart and text): Elise F. Jones, et al., *Teenage Pregnancy in Industrialized Countries. A Study Sponsored by the Alan Guttmacher Institute* (New Haven: Yale University Press, 1986), pp. 24–30, 251–55; Alan Guttmacher Institute, *Facts in Brief: Teenage Sexual and Reproductive Behavior in the United States* (New York: AGI, 1991).

INFANT AND CHILD HEALTH

- **We're Number One in infant mortality.**
- **We're Number One in percentage of infants born at low birth weight.**

The U.S. infant mortality rate of 10 deaths per 1,000 live births is the highest of the nineteen major industrial countries.[41] Our rate is more than twice as high as Japan's and 25 percent higher than the average rate for the nineteen major industrial nations. Infant mortality is one of the primary indicators used by the United Nations, the World Health Organization, and other international agencies to assess a nation's health. Our Number One showing in this area should be a major cause for concern.

The death of an infant usually occurs because of poor health conditions that predate birth. Low birth weight (under 5.5 pounds) is often due to insufficient prenatal care or drug use; babies born at low birth weight are twenty times more likely than others to die within the first year of life and forty times more likely to die within the first month. Not surprisingly, the United States is Number One in low birth weight as well as infant mortality. The two indicators paint a symmetrical portrait of infant and child health in the most developed nations: Japan and the Scandinavian nations are uniformly the best performers and the United States is consistently the worst.

Low birth weight in the United States is most prevalent among infants of impoverished, inner-city mothers. Because these women have little or no access to prenatal care, they miss out on vital medical attention and counseling. Many are unaware that the use and abuse of tobacco, alcohol, and drugs during pregnancy can cause Fetal Alcohol Syndrome, cocaine dependence, and other conditions that endanger their infant's physical, emotional, and intellectual development. In America, prenatal care is a privilege, while "in Europe or Canada, no pregnant woman has to ask how, or where, she will receive prenatal care, or who will pay for it," according to a U.S. congressman. "No child is denied preventive health care . . . because of an inability to pay."[42]

Seven percent of American children are born at low birth weight (about one infant every eleven minutes).[43] Twenty-six nations, including Egypt, Jordan, Romania, and the former Soviet Union, do better. How do we explain our concurrent medical advancement and backwardness? Largely by looking at contradictions within our health care system. America's high rates of infant mortality and low birth weight are largely caused by large discrepancies in these rates within our country along geographic, class, and racial lines. About 60 percent of black and Hispanic women receive early prenatal care, compared to 80 percent of white women.[44] Black infants in Chicago, Detroit, and Philadelphia have a greater chance of dying within their first year than do infants born in Jamaica, Costa Rica, or Chile. The mortality rate throughout America for black infants is 18 per 1,000, double the rate for white infants, 9.2 per 1,000.[45] In

Washington, D.C., 13.5 percent of black babies are born at low birth weight, a larger percentage than for infants born in Mauritania, Lesotho, Mongolia, and Thailand.

While the infant mortality rate has improved throughout the world in recent years, the United States is slipping relative to its competitors. In 1960, America's infant mortality rate was about 26 per 1,000 live births. Italy, Belgium, Spain, Ireland, Germany, France, Austria, Canada, and Japan all had higher infant mortality rates. Now, their infant mortality rates are lower than that of the United States. Consequently, we've earned the ignoble Number One spot in death of babies before their first birthday.

Infant mortality rates per 1,000 live births for the nineteen major industrial countries, 1989 and 1960:

COUNTRY	1989 RATE	1960 RATE
United States	**10**	**26**
New Zealand	10	23
Italy	10	44
Belgium	10	31
Spain	9	47
Ireland	9	31
Germany	8	33
United Kingdom	8	23
Norway	8	19
France	8	29
Denmark	8	22
Austria	8	37
Australia	8	21
Switzerland	7	22
Netherlands	7	18
Canada	7	28
Sweden	6	16
Finland	6	22
Japan	4	31

Sources (for chart and text): UNICEF, *The State of the World's Children 1991* (New York: Oxford University Press, 1991), pp. 102–105. Children's Defense Fund, *The State of America's Children, 1991* (Washington, D.C.: CDF, 1991), pp. 17, 166.

Percentage of infants born at low birth weight, 1980–88:

COUNTRY	LOW BIRTH WEIGHT[46]	COUNTRY	LOW BIRTH WEIGHT
United States	**7**	Egypt	5
United Kingdom	7	France	5
Australia	6	Hong Kong	5
Austria	6	Iran	5
Bulgaria	6	Japan	5
Canada	6	Jordan	5
Czechoslovakia	6	New Zealand	5
Denmark	6	Portugal	5
Germany (unified)	6	Switzerland	5
Greece	6	Finland	4
Romania	6	Ireland	4
Saudi Arabia	6	Norway	4
USSR	6	Sweden	4
Belgium	5	Spain	1

Source: UNICEF, *The State of the World's Children 1991* (New York: Oxford University Press, 1991), p. 104.

- **We're Number One in preschoolers NOT fully immunized against polio and other diseases.**
- **We're Number One in death of children younger than five.**

Just as the United States leads the nineteen major industrial nations in infant mortality, we're first in the rate of mortality for children under five. Poverty, neglect, and inadequate health care have put many young American children at risk of sickness, injury, and even death. More than forty thousand infants born this year—12 per 1,000—will die within five years. Again, as with infant mortality, Japan has the lowest rate of death for those under five, 6 per 1,000 births, or half that of the United States.

The United States leads in deaths of children under five due to preventable causes such as fire and homicide. Childhood diseases that appeared to have been conquered years ago are also reappearing in menacing proportions. Whooping cough (pertussis) cases have doubled among children age 1 to 4 since 1970.

Cases of measles are rising at an alarming rate, from 1,500 in 1983 to nearly 28,000 in 1990. Three Americans died of measles in 1988; eighty-nine died (forty-nine of them preschoolers) in 1990. In the first three months of 1991, New York City reported as many measles cases as in all of 1990. Mumps, tetanus, and rubella are on the rise as well.

There is a simple explanation for these increases: lack of immunization. "Immunization rates among U.S. white children are well below those for children in all other compared countries; rates for U.S. racial minorities are considerably lower still," says the American Academy of Pediatrics.[47] From 1982 to 1990, the cost of fully immunizing a child rose tenfold, from $6.69 to $70.49. Nearly half the parents surveyed in a 1991 poll say America's children are not being immunized because the process is too expensive. Yet for every dollar we spend on immunizations for children, ten dollars is saved in later medical costs, according to the Children's Defense Fund.[48] For example, it would have cost just $37,000 to immunize the children who were treated—at a cost of over $2.5 million—for whooping cough in forty-six U.S. children's hospitals in 1988. In Denmark, France, Germany, Norway, and the United Kingdom, vaccinations are free and nearly all children are immunized.

American health officials are aware of the immunization crisis and have called on the government to increase funding for vaccinations, especially in inner-city areas. While the government has promised to increase funds, in June 1991 President Bush deferred an emergency plan that would have provided an additional $91 million to buy and distribute vaccines to cities and states.[49]

Percentage of preschool children with full polio, DTP (diphtheria-tetanus-pertussis), and measles immunizations, 1985–87:[50]

COUNTRY	POLIO	DTP	MEASLES
Denmark	100.0	94.0[51]	82.0
Belgium	99.0	95.0	90.0
France	97.0	97.0	55.0
Germany	95.0	95.0	50.0
Netherlands	96.9	96.9	92.8
Switzerland[52]	95.0	90.0	60.0
United Kingdom[53]	87.0	87.0	76.0
Norway	80.0	80.0	87.0
Spain	80.0	88.0	83.0
United States	**55.3**	**64.9**	**60.8**
U.S. nonwhite	**40.1**	**48.7**	**48.8**

Sources (for chart and text): Bret C. Williams and C. Arden Miller, *Preventive Health Care for Young Children* (Arlington, Va.: National Center for Clinical Infant Programs, 1991), p. 76; Bret C. Williams, "Immunization Coverage Among Preschool Children: The United States and Selected European Countries," *Pediatrics* (Elk Grove Village, Ill.: American Academy of Pediatrics, 1990), p. 1052; various releases and publications of the American Academy of Pediatrics, Elk Grove Village, Ill.

Deaths of children under five per 1,000 live births, 1989:

COUNTRY	DEATH RATE	COUNTRY	DEATH RATE
United States	**12**	Australia	9
Belgium	12	Canada	9
New Zealand	12	East Germany	9
Ireland	11	France	9
Italy	11	Switzerland	9
Austria	10	Hong Kong	8
Denmark	10	Netherlands	8
Norway	10	Finland	7
Spain	10	Sweden	7
West Germany	10	Japan	6
United Kingdom	10		

Source: UNICEF, *The State of the World's Children 1991* (New York: Oxford University Press, 1991), p. 104.

AIDS AND CANCER

• **We're Number One in AIDS.**

The United States has had nearly ten times as many reported AIDS cases as Uganda, the nation with the second most cases, and the cumulative rate of AIDS is higher in the United States than in any developed nation. In per capita terms, we have experienced 3 times as many AIDS cases as Switzerland, 10 times as many as the United Kingdom, and 270 times as many as Japan. While three developing African countries—Uganda, Malawi, and the Congo—have a higher cumulative AIDS rate than the general American population, AIDS has been more prevalent in the nonwhite U.S. population than in these three African nations.

Though attempts are made to accurately update the number of officially reported AIDS cases, the World Health Organization acknowledges widespread underreporting. Therefore, while the official world count as of October 1991 was 418,403 cases since the disease first appeared, the cumulative number of AIDS cases is probably closer to 900,000 for adults and 400,000 for infants and children.[54]

The first decade of AIDS that ended in 1991 was just the beginning. Millions of people throughout the world, including at least one million Americans, are infected with HIV, the virus that causes AIDS. By the year 2000, the World Health Organization predicts that forty million people worldwide will be infected with HIV.[55] Unless some miracle cure is found, these forty million people will die of AIDS. More than 130,000 Americans have died already. By the end of 1993, as many as 480,000 Americans will have developed AIDS and as many as 340,000 will have died from it, according to the Centers for Disease Control.[56]

Until recently, many HIV-positive individuals in the United States were not classified as having AIDS simply because the definition of the disease was outdated. The U.S. Centers for Disease Control, after criticism from medical groups and AIDS activists, revised its definition of AIDS so that these HIV-positive Americans, many of whom are women, now receive disability benefits for which they were not eligible before. Though the U.S. share of all reported AIDS cases is falling, it still amounts to about half of the known cases, despite the fact that Americans make up about 5 percent of the world's population.

Cumulative number of officially reported AIDS cases and cumulative rate per 100,000 population, as of 1991:[57]

COUNTRY	TOTAL CASES	CUMULATIVE RATE PER 100,000
U.S. nonwhite	**93,569**	**155.7**
Malawi	12,074	131.8
Uganda	21,719	120.9
Congo	2,405	107.3
United States	**202,843**	**81.0**
Switzerland	1,891	28.0
France	15,534	27.6
Spain	9,112	23.2
Canada	5,228	19.7
Australia	2,678	15.8
Italy	9,792	17.0
Denmark	842	16.4
Netherlands	1,799	12.0
Belgium	896	9.0
Germany (unified)	6,708	8.5
New Zealand	274	8.3
United Kingdom	4,758	8.3
Austria	594	7.8
Sweden	587	6.9
Ireland	205	5.9
Norway	220	5.2
Finland	88	1.8
Japan	405	0.3

Sources: World Health Organization, Global Programme on AIDS (October, 1991); U.S. figures: U.S. Centers for Disease Control "HIV/AIDS Surveillance," December, 1991, p. 9.

Casualties of war.

Fourteen Americans were killed in combat in the first thirty days of the 1991 Persian Gulf war; during the same period, AIDS claimed the lives of 2,500 Americans. The equivalent of the federal government's entire research budget for AIDS in 1989, $981 million, was spent in approximately two days of the ground war.

Sources: "AIDS—the Second Decade," *The New York Times*, June 5, 1991; National Center for Health Statistics, *Health, United States, 1990* (Hyattsville, Md.: Public Health Service, 1991), p. 200; Congressional Budget Office.

- **We're Number One in thinking that a person with AIDS can transmit the disease by coughing or sneezing on someone.**
- **We're Number One in percentage of people who say they would refuse to work alongside someone with AIDS.**

These grim facts indicate that while the United States is Number One in AIDS, we're far from being Number One in AIDS awareness, and we're among the most biased toward people with AIDS among the nineteen major industrial nations.[58] One quarter of Americans surveyed say that being coughed or sneezed on by a person with AIDS is "a likely way to catch AIDS," and one quarter say they would "refuse to work alongside someone who has AIDS." Additionally, more than half of the Americans surveyed say that generally it is a person's own fault if he or she gets AIDS. The United States is also Number One among the nineteen major industrial nations in percentage of people who are "very concerned" about getting AIDS (20 percent) and Number One in people who said that "despite the risk of AIDS, I have not changed my behavior" (15 percent).

Source: Survey Research Consultants International, *Index to International Public Opinion, 1987–1988* (New York: Greenwood Press, 1989), p. 585–90. Poll conducted by Gallup International Research Institutes.

• We're Number One in incidence of cancer among men.

Men in the United States have a higher cancer rate than men in any other nation for which data is available. The rate among American women is also among the highest in the world. As many as four men in ten and three women in ten who live an average-length life will get cancer before they die. For black men, rates are even higher.

More than one million cases of cancer are diagnosed each year, according to the American Cancer Society.[59] Prostate cancer is the most common cancer among men, breast cancer the most common among women. For both sexes, lung cancer is the most deadly, taking an estimated 143,000 lives in 1991.

Among the major industrial nations, Italy, France, and New Zealand have cancer rates that are comparable to that of the United States. Lower rates are found in Spain and Japan. Mortality rates due to cancer are higher in many countries than in the United States because of early detection and relatively high survival rates among Americans. Still, doctors don't know exactly why cancer rates are highest in America.

"I don't think you can draw definite conclusions about why we have higher cancer rates," says Dr. Mark Baptiste, director of the New York State Cancer Registry. "The increase in incidence is in part due to better monitoring, but there is much we don't know."[60] Until cancer is better understood, doctors are recommending what they *do* know: that patients who exercise, eat well, and don't smoke have a better chance of remaining healthy.

Percentage (range) of male and female population living to age 74 that will get cancer, 1978–82:[61]

COUNTRY	MALE RANGE (%)	FEMALE RANGE (%)
U.S. black	**41.0–47.7**	**24.0–28.4**
U.S. white	**29.6–39.9**	**23.7–33.7**
France	29.3–39.7	17.9–22.7
New Zealand[62]	30.2–39.4	25.2–34.1
Italy	22.0–38.7	15.9–22.3
Switzerland	30.4–37.0	20.7–25.8
Germany	28.3–36.7	21.2–25.0
Canada	25.8–36.0	20.6–29.0
Australia	27.6–35.7	20.6–26.4
Netherlands	35.3	23.0
United Kingdom	24.4–34.3	20.6–26.6
Denmark	30.5	26.8
Japan	25.4–30.4	15.0–18.8
Finland	30.0	19.1
Spain	20.3–28.3	13.3–16.9
Norway	24.8–27.3	21.4–25.2
Sweden	26.4	24.7
Ireland	22.4	20.3

Source: Calum Muir et al., eds., *Cancer Incidence on Five Continents* (Lyon: International Agency for Research on Cancer, 1987), 5:936–37.

- **We're Number One in incidence of breast cancer.**
- **We're Number 13 in death due to breast cancer.**

The United States has the highest incidence of breast cancer among women of all countries for which data is available, and our rate is climbing. One woman in nine will get breast cancer sometime during her lifetime, according to the American Cancer Society.

Increased efforts to identify breast cancer in its earliest stages may partially explain why our recorded breast cancer rate is the highest. Yet one recent report by the Democratic Study Group charges that America is *not* at the forefront in early detection: "Despite the higher incidence of breast cancer, there is no effort in the United States to promote the early detection of breast cancer comparable to the efforts now under way in Western Europe."[63] Sweden's program, according to the report, is so advanced that all women from age 40 to 74 receive letters in the mail scheduling them for a mammogram.

Forty-four thousand American women died of breast cancer in 1991, almost a 100 percent increase since 1960 when 23,755 women died. Breast cancer is now the leading killer of women age 35 to 54. Despite these bleak facts, three quarters of the American women diagnosed with breast cancer today survive for at least five years. Therefore, while we're Number One in incidence, we're only thirteenth in death due to breast cancer among the nineteen major industrial nations.

Percentage (range) of women living to age 74 that will get breast cancer, 1978–82, and deaths due to breast cancer per 100,000 women, 1987–89:[64]

COUNTRY	INCIDENCE RANGE (%)	DEATHS PER 100,000
United States	**7.4–9.9**	**33.5**
New Zealand	6.3–9.3	36.3
Canada	5.2–8.3	34.1
Switzerland	6.6–8.2	46.2
Netherlands	8.0	44.0
Australia	5.2–7.8	28.4
United Kingdom	6.0–7.1	53.4
France	5.4–7.0	34.8
Denmark	6.9	50.8
Sweden	6.8	—
Germany	5.5–6.7	45.7
Italy	5.2–6.6	35.5
Ireland	6.5	34.7
Norway	5.2–6.4	36.1
Spain	3.7–5.0	23.2
Finland	4.9	30.3
Japan	1.9–3.0	9.2

Sources: Calum Muir et. al., eds., *Cancer Incidence on Five Continents* (Lyon: International Agency for Research on Cancer, 1987), 5:882–83; World Health Organization, *World Health Statistics Annual 1990* (Geneva: WHO, 1991). For text: Catherine C. Boring, Teresa S. Squires, Tony Tong, "Cancer Statistics, 1991," *Ca-A Cancer Journal for Clinicians*, vol. 41, no. 1, January/February 1991; Democratic Study Group, "Why Conservatives Don't Talk About America's Health System," Special Report, No. 102–6, May 24, 1991, pp. 49–52.

MALPRACTICE

- **We're Number One in medical malpractice lawsuits.**
- **We're Number One in cesarean section births per delivery.**

"There's definitely been an effect on cesarean sections as a result of litigation," says Morton Lebow, spokesman for the American College of Obstetricians and Gynecologists. "Three-quarters of our doctors have been sued at least once," and some have been

sued multiple times, Lebow adds.[65] More than half of all sur-
geons and a third of all physicians have incurred liability claims
during their careers, according to the American Medical Association, and malpractice claims increased about 10 percent a year
between 1975 and 1985. Insurance premiums for obstetricians
have risen to almost $40,000 a year on average, and as high as
$100,000 annually in some areas. There are approximately six
teen malpractice claims filed per hundred physicians annually in
the United States, as much as five times the amount in Canada
and the United Kingdom.[66]

This glut of malpractice suits has led some doctors to stop
delivering babies, leaving some poor and rural areas of America
with no obstetrical care, according to a study of the National
Academy of Sciences' Institute of Medicine.[67] It has also caused
doctors to perform millions of unnecessary cesarean sections as
"defensive medicine," in order to "fend off charges that [they]
had not done everything they could."[68] In a cesarean section
birth, the baby is removed surgically from the uterus, and there
is generally less chance of complications than in a normal vaginal
birth. Almost one in four births in the United States is done by
cesarean section, nearly three times the rate in Japan.

Cesarean sections per 100 births, 1983–89:

COUNTRY	CESAREAN SECTIONS	COUNTRY	CESAREAN SECTIONS
United States	24	Sweden	12
Canada	19	Netherlands	11
Australia	16	New Zealand	11
Finland	15	United Kingdom[69]	10
Denmark	13	Ireland	9
France	13	Japan	9
Norway	13	Austria	8
Spain	12	Belgium	8

Sources: Organization for Economic Cooperation and Development (Paris), Health Data file, 1991;
Francis C. Norton, Paul J. Placek, and Selma M. Taffel, "Comparisons of National Cesarean–Section
Rates," *The New England Journal of Medicine*, vol. 316, no. 7, February 12, 1987, p. 387.

DIET

- **We're Number One in beef consumption per capita.**
- **We're Number One in coronary bypass operations per capita.**

Red meat is on its way out, for both health and cost reasons, according to conventional wisdom. The beef industry has even resorted to flashy ad campaigns to save its product. Still, while consumption is dropping, Americans continue to eat a good portion of their own weight in red meat each year. In fact, the United States consumes more beef per capita than any of the nineteen major industrial nations.[70]

At the same time, perhaps not coincidentally, we're Number One in coronary bypass operations per capita. In 1987, the most recent year for which data is available, 332,000 coronary by-passes were performed in the United States. In per capita terms, our bypass rate (1,360 per million population) is more than twice that of Australia, the nation with the second highest rate (519 per million).[71] Coronary bypasses are performed in order to alleviate the effects of arteriosclerosis (blockage of arteries) caused by poor health and diet, including consumption of—you guessed it—red meat.

Annual beef consumption, pounds per capita, 1988–90:[72]

COUNTRY	BEEF CONSUMPTION	COUNTRY	BEEF CONSUMPTION
United States	**97.2**	Switzerland	55.6
Australia	88.9	Germany	50.3
Canada	86.2	Netherlands	42.5
New Zealand	79.6	Ireland	41.1
France	63.7	Norway	38.9
Italy	58.9	Japan	17.2

Sources: U.S. Bureau of the Census, *Statistical Abstract of the United States 1991* (Washington, D.C.: USGPO, 1991), p. 843; *European Marketing Data and Statistics 1991* (London: Euromonitor Publications, 1991), p. 328; *International Marketing Data and Statistics 1991* (London: Euromonitor Publications, 1991), p. 428.

• We're Number One in snack food consumption.

From potato chips to pretzels, popcorn to pork rinds, the United States leads in snack food consumption among all countries for which data is available. Americans eat almost twenty pounds of snacks a year, five times as much as the healthy Scandinavian countries, and twice as much as the British (they prefer biscuits, of course).

Within the United States, New Englanders are the snack kings, with 24.4 pounds of annual consumption per capita, five pounds more than the national average. Southerners, however, have the pork rind market covered; they eat more than seven times as much of these savory treats as New England residents.

The repercussions of American snackmania? More than one quarter of American adults are overweight (26.2 percent) and have high serum cholesterol (28 percent).[73] We're in the top three in calorie consumption, the top four in fat, and the bottom five in iron consumption among the nineteen major industrial nations. The effect on overall health is apparent when one considers that each day Japan's citizens consume half as much fat, 800 fewer calories (that's a small meal), and more iron than Americans—and they live longer, healthier lives.

Pounds of snack food consumed per capita annually, 1987–91:

COUNTRY	POUNDS PER CAPITA	COUNTRY	POUNDS PER CAPITA
United States	**19.2**	Japan	3.7
Italy	17.6	Denmark	3.5
United Kingdom	10.0	Spain	2.9
Norway	8.0	Switzerland	2.7
Germany	6.1	Netherlands	2.5
Australia	4.4	Finland	2.2
Sweden	4.4		

Source: *Snack World* magazine, various issues, published by the Snack Food Association (Alexandria, Va.).

Average number of calories and grams of fat consumed per capita per day, 1986–88:

COUNTRY	CALORIES	FAT
Belgium	3901	199.8
Ireland	3688	148.1
United States	**3644**	**163.5**
Switzerland	3623	169.6
Denmark	3605	176.0
Italy	3571	144.4
Germany	3528	152.6
Spain	3494	150.7
New Zealand	3476	143.9
Austria	3474	161.8
Canada	3451	152.2
Australia	3347	136.7
France	3312	141.8
Netherlands	3303	152.3
Norway	3266	136.7
United Kingdom	3259	145.6
Finland	3120	128.6
Sweden	3031	131.1
Japan	2822	80.2

Source: Food and Agriculture Organization of the United Nations, *Production Yearbook* (Rome: FAO, 1990), pp. 289–94.

DOCTORS

• **We're Number One in physicians' salaries.**

The United States boasts some of the finest physicians in the world and some of the highest-paid ones as well. The average American physician makes $155,800 a year, more than five times the annual salary of the average American. By this standard, doctors make more in America than in any of the nineteen major industrial nations. Japan's doctors, by the same comparison, make about half as much as American doctors. In Ireland, doctors barely make more than the average citizen.

Ratio of average physician's income to average employee income, 1986–89:[74]

COUNTRY	RATIO	COUNTRY	RATIO
United States	**5.45**	Australia	2.16
Germany	4.29	Denmark	2.03
Switzerland	4.10	Sweden	1.80
Canada	3.74	Finland	1.75
France	3.27	Norway	1.29
New Zealand	3.06	Italy	1.10
Japan	2.46	Ireland	1.07
United Kingdom	2.42		

Sources: Organization for Economic Cooperation and Development, *Health Care Systems in Transition* (Paris: OECD, 1990), pp. 142, 200; OECD Health Data file, 1991.

Is there a doctor in the house?

While American doctors are well paid, access to physicians is another matter entirely. The United States is eighth in doctors per capita and tenth in number of annual contacts with a physician among the nineteen major industrial nations. Spain, Germany, Norway, and Sweden have 3 or more practicing physicians per 1,000 population, compared to 2.3 per 1,000 in the United States. The Japanese, Germans, and Italians consult doctors the most—more than ten times per year. That's about twice as often as Americans, 22 percent of whom say they haven't seen a doctor in more than a year.[75]

Sources: Organization for Economic Cooperation and Development, *Health Care Systems in Transition* (Paris: OECD, 1990), pp. 151, 155; OECD Health Data file, 1991.

PIETIES AND PRIORITIES

FAMILY, RELIGION, SEX, SPORTS, AND VICE

The United States is a nation wed to religion, plagued by fragmented families, and consumed by sports. American values are increasingly traditional and conservative relative to those of other nations. Only 22 percent of Americans say they would welcome more sexual freedom, while 89 percent say they would appreciate more respect for authority.[1] Yet often what we say contradicts what we do.

Trying to describe the American character is a near-impossible task because there is no set group of values or behaviors that we all share. Contradictions may be explained by the fact that the United States is really a conglomerate of many nations: urban and rural, black and white, rich and poor, traditional and progressive. We can, however, glean certain insights about America's pieties and priorities—our beliefs and behaviors—and how we compare with other nations in such diverse areas as death and divorce, smoking and single-parent families, God and golf.

MARRIAGE AND DIVORCE

- **We're Number One in marriage.**
- **We're Number One in still believing in marriage.**
- **We're Number One in divorce.**

Each year, 2.4 million Americans join together in holy matrimony, and each year 1.2 million split apart in some state of acrimony. Marriage in America is at best a delicate institution, at worst a vestige of a bygone era. Yet only 9 percent of Americans, the smallest number of any of the nineteen major industrial nations surveyed, say they think marriage is outdated. Are we fooling ourselves?[2]

The United States leads the nineteen major industrial nations in marriage, but we're also Number One in divorce. About one half of American marriages end in divorce today.[3] The U.S. divorce rate (4.8 per 1,000 population annually) is twice as high as Germany's, more than three times that of Japan, and twelve times that of Italy. At the same time, Americans are less tolerant of divorce than most of the nineteen major industrial nations. Eighty-two percent of the French, 80 percent of the British, and 77 percent of Germans say divorce can be justified, compared to 73 percent of Americans.[4]

Times have changed in some respects and not in others: the marriage rate in 1900 was 9.3 per 1,000, compared to 9.7 per 1,000 now. The divorce rate in 1900 was 0.7 per 1,000, compared to 4.8 per 1,000 now.[5] In other words, the divorce rate has increased sevenfold while the marriage rate has essentially stayed the same. Unfortunately, America's high divorce rate is likely to continue. A recent study shows that children of divorced parents are four times as likely to become divorced as are other children—and the United States is Number One in children involved in divorce.[6] Is this necessarily bad? "Increased divorce rates in the United States can be interpreted as an index of social decay," says Joseph Nye, "or as evidence of increased opportunity for women and men to escape hopeless situations that they previously had to endure."[7]

Marriage and divorce rate per 1,000 population, 1988–89:

COUNTRY	MARRIAGE RATE	DIVORCE RATE[8]
United States	**9.7**	**4.8**
Soviet Union	9.4	3.4
Canada	7.2	3.1
Australia	7.1	2.4
New Zealand	7.1	2.6
Switzerland	6.9	1.9
United Kingdom	6.9	2.9
Germany	6.5	2.1
Denmark	6.3	3.0
Netherlands	6.0	1.9
Belgium	5.8	1.9
Japan	5.8	1.3
Italy	5.5	0.4
Finland	5.3	2.9
Spain	5.3	—
Sweden	5.2	2.3
Ireland	5.1	—
France	4.9	1.9
Norway	4.9	2.1
Austria	4.7	2.0

Sources: United Nations, *Demographic Yearbook, 1989* (New York: United Nations, 1991); *Information Please Almanac, 1992* (Boston: Houghton Mifflin, 1992), p. 135.

• We're Number One in single-parent families.

It's not surprising, given America's high divorce rate, that we have the most single-parent families of any nation for which data is available. More than a quarter of our families with dependent children are headed by a single parent; in the clear majority of cases that parent is a woman.[9] In relative terms, America has more than twice as many single-parent families as Germany and five times as many as Japan. Our rate doubled between 1970 and 1984, the most recent year for which data are available.

The perception of single-parent families as unintended and

impoverished is largely correct; 54 percent of poor children in America live in female-headed families.[10] Yet, increasingly, women (and men) who are not married are choosing to raise children on their own.

Percentage of all families with dependent children that are led by a single parent, 1980–84:

COUNTRY	PERCENTAGE	COUNTRY	PERCENTAGE
United States	**26.0**	Switzerland	12.0
Sweden	14.2	Germany	11.4
United Kingdom[11]	13.0	France	10.2
Belgium	12.3	Ireland	7.1
Netherlands	12.3	Japan	5.1

Source: Organization for Economic Cooperation and Development, *Lone-Parent Families* (Paris: OECD, 1990), p. 29.

AUTHORITY

- **We're Number One in saying that more emphasis on family life would be a good thing.**
- **We're Number One in saying that more respect for authority would be a good thing.**

Responding perhaps to what Allan Bloom and other conservative critics have described as a nation plagued by moral chaos, Americans are longing for more family structure and respect for authority. While all nations surveyed express hardy approval of a rejuvenated family life, the United States is the most emphatic of the nineteen major industrial nations. Ninety-five percent of Americans approve of an increased focus on family, 4 percent of Americans are ambivalent, and 1 percent think it is all a bad idea.

As for being Number One in advocating greater respect for authority, Thomas Jefferson was right from the start when he suggested: "All authority belongs to the people."[12]

Percentage of population who say more emphasis on family life would be good, and percentage who say greater respect for authority would be good, 1981–83:[13]

COUNTRY	FAMILY EMPHASIS	RESPECT AUTHORITY
United States	**94.9**	**85.0**
Finland	94.8	29.0
Norway	92.2	36.3
Ireland	90.5	84.4
Australia	90.2	68.3
Canada	90.2	75.6
Denmark	88.0	35.9
France	87.9	56.8
Italy	87.9	61.9
Belgium	84.0	60.0
Sweden	83.7	31.5
Germany	83.5	38.9
Spain	83.5	76.0
United Kingdom[14]	82.1	70.0
Japan	79.7	6.5
Netherlands	70.4	56.9

Source: World Values Survey.

Enough already.

By reputation, Japan is one of the most ordered societies in the world, a nation where respect for authority plays an integral role in all social interaction. Apparently, the Japanese have reached their threshold. While thirteen of fifteen Americans surveyed favor more respect for authority, only one in fifteen Japanese respondents say the same. Ninety-four percent say they've had enough.

Source: World Values Survey.

BELIEF IN GOD

- **We're Number One in belief in God.**
- **We're Number One in belief in the devil.**
- **We're Number One in belief in heaven.**
- **We're Number One in belief in hell.**

"How can I believe in God," asks Woody Allen, "when just last week I got my tongue caught in the roller of an electric typewriter?"[15] Atheists and agnostics may have more profound reasons to doubt divinity, but 98 percent of Americans say they believe in God.

Belief in God is more widespread in America than in any of the nineteen major industrial nations, as is belief in the devil, heaven, and hell. Nine in ten Americans believe in heaven, while seven in ten believe in the devil and hell. Only two Americans out of one hundred say they don't believe in God. Sweden is the least believing in God; Denmark is the most skeptical toward the devil, heaven, and hell. All nations are more accepting of God and heaven than the devil and hell. For example, four times as many Germans believe in God as in the devil, and twice as many believe in heaven as in hell.

While the United States is also Number One in belief in "a soul," Japan is Number One in belief in reincarnation. Fifty-one percent of Japanese respondents say they believe in reincarnation, compared to 28.5 percent of Americans.

Percentage of population who say they believe in God, the devil, heaven, and hell, 1981–83:

COUNTRY	GOD	DEVIL	HEAVEN	HELL
United States	**98**	**70**	**90**	**73**
Ireland	97	62	89	59
Canada	93	44	75	42
Spain	92	38	56	38
Italy	88	33	44	33
Belgium	86	24	41	21
Australia	85	42	64	40
United Kingdom[16]	81	34	62	29
Germany	80	18	34	15
Norway	73	30	49	23
Netherlands	71	22	44	16
France	65	18	27	15
Denmark	63	12	17	8
Japan	62	22	37	29
Sweden	60	13	32	11

Source: World Values Survey.

Children of God.

In most countries, there is a large gap between youth and old age when it comes to ranking God's importance, but in America, piety is not lost across the generations. When asked to rank the importance of God in their lives, half to three quarters of young people surveyed in Denmark, France, Germany, Japan, Netherlands, and the U.K. say God has little importance in their lives. Only 10 percent of American youth say this. In another survey, 93 percent of young Americans report that religion is important to them, compared to 39 percent in Germany and 38 percent in Japan.

Sources: Ronald Inglehart, *Culture Shift in Advanced Industrial Society* (Princeton: Princeton University Press, 1990), p. 188; Survey Research Consultants International, *Index to International Public Opinion, 1988–89* (New York: Greenwood Press, 1990), pp. 610, 622.

THE MEANING OF LIFE

- **We're Number One in thinking about the meaning of life.**
- **We're Number One in thinking about death.**

The French had Sartre, the Germans had Heidegger, and the Danes had Kierkegaard, but Americans are the people most consumed with existential thought these days. Five out of ten Americans say they often think about the meaning of life; three in ten say they think about it sometimes. Sartre's French compatriots are a close second to the Americans in pondering why we're here. The Swedes, perhaps content to let Bergman's films do the philosophizing, are last. On the gloomier side, the United States and Italy share the Number One spot in thinking about death.

The results of our extensive thinking about life and death are surprisingly optimistic. Only 20 percent of Americans feel that life is meaningless, less than in twelve of the sixteen nations surveyed. Inhabitants of the Netherlands, Sweden, and Norway are most optimistic, while the Spanish are the most likely to feel that life is meaningless.

Percentage of population saying they "often" or "sometimes" think about the meaning and purpose of life, and about death, and percentage who "often" or "sometimes" feel that life is meaningless, 1981–83:

COUNTRY	THINK ABOUT LIFE	THINK ABOUT DEATH	THINK LIFE IS MEANINGLESS
United States	**82.7**	**65.1**	**20.2**
France	81.1	56.7	35.1
Canada	80.7	60.8	23.9
Italy	78.1	65.1	35.3
Japan	77.0	55.2	26.9
Finland	76.8	59.7	23.1
Australia	75.9	61.9	24.0
Denmark	71.8	51.1	21.3
Germany	69.9	53.0	27.8
Norway	69.8	52.9	19.1
Netherlands	66.7	54.1	17.2
Spain	66.7	59.0	43.6
United Kingdom[17]	66.7	56.7	26.6
Belgium	65.8	46.6	25.4
Ireland	64.9	55.2	25.6
Sweden	64.4	51.6	18.6

Source: World Values Survey.

• **We're Number One in percentage of population willing to fight for their country.**

"If a country is worth living in," said Manning Coles, "it is worth fighting for."[18] America agrees, more so than any of the nineteen major industrial nations, according to a recent survey. Seventy-seven percent of American respondents answer yes when asked whether they would be willing to fight for their nation if a war occurred.[19]

Americans are also more willing to go to war than the Soviet Union (63 percent), South Africa (66 percent), and Colombia (53 percent). Only Israel, which technically has been in a state of war since 1948, is more willing to fight—89 percent say they would defend their country if necessary. Japan has the most pacifists, with only 6 percent of those surveyed saying they would fight for their country.

Percentage of population who say they would fight in a war for their country, the nineteen major industrial nations, 1989:

COUNTRY	WILLING TO FIGHT	COUNTRY	WILLING TO FIGHT
United States	**77**	New Zealand	38
Finland	66	Italy	34
Denmark	62	Switzerland	32
Australia	60	Belgium	21
United Kingdom	49	Austria	17
Canada	44	Germany	15
France	41	Japan	6
Netherlands	40		

Source: Survey Research Consultants International, *Index to International Public Opinion 1989–1990* (New York: Greenwood Press, 1991), pp. 665–76.

• We're Number One in percentage of people who think it is all right to keep money that they have found.

It's a classic morality test: you find some cash lying on the street. Do you try to find its rightful owner? Give it to someone who you think needs it? Or just pocket it? If the latter is your answer, you won't receive much scorn from Americans, more than half of whom say it is justifiable, at least sometimes, to keep money that one has found. In fact, more Americans think it is fair to pocket the cash than do the inhabitants of the remaining nineteen major industrial nations. Most righteous are the Norwegians, 77 percent of whom say it is *never* right to keep money you have found.

Percentage of population who say keeping money that you have found can sometimes or always be justified, 1981–83:

COUNTRY	OKAY TO KEEP MONEY	COUNTRY	OKAY TO KEEP MONEY
United States	**57.2**	France	37.9
Spain	56.9	Finland	36.4
Canada	50.6	Denmark	35.6
Belgium	47.7	Italy	34.7
Australia	46.7	United Kingdom[20]	31.1
Netherlands	46.4	Sweden	28.1
Ireland	42.4	Japan	27.2
Germany	38.8	Norway	23.1

Source: World Values Survey.

SMOKING AND DRINKING

• **We're Number 2 in cigarette consumption.**

Only the Japanese smoke more cigarettes than do Americans among the nineteen major industrial nations. On average, Americans smoke more than two thousand cigarettes a year, a little less than six a day. But since only about one third of Americans smoke—a smaller percentage than in many of the nations listed in the chart—average cigarette consumption for smokers is actually closer to a pack (twenty cigarettes) a day. The healthiest nation of the bunch are the Norwegians, who smoke a third fewer cigarettes per capita than we do.

Number of cigarettes consumed per person, the nineteen major industrial nations, 1986–88:

COUNTRY	CIGARETTES PER PERSON	COUNTRY	CIGARETTES PER PERSON
Japan	2,537	Belgium	1,791
United States	**2,100**	United Kingdom	1,695
Canada	2,055	France	1,683
Switzerland	1,997	Ireland	1,519
Spain	1,982	Finland	1,515
Austria	1,914	Denmark	1,350
Germany	1,906	Sweden	1,334
Australia	1,900	Netherlands	1,154
New Zealand	1,815	Norway	639

Source: *The Economist Book of Vital World Statistics* (New York: Times Books, 1990), p. 239.

- **We're Number 4 in alcohol consumption per capita.**

Spain, Finland, and Canada are the only nations that drink more hard alcohol per capita than the United States among the nineteen major industrial nations. American hard alcohol consumption peaked in 1974 at 3.2 liters per person annually, and is now about 2.5 liters per person; beer consumption has remained relatively stable, while wine consumption has increased. Americans drink about twice as much alcohol as Australians, though the Aussies outdo us in beer and wine consumption. Per person, Germans drink the most beer, and the Italians and French consume the most wine. However, alcohol consumption in Eastern European nations—Hungary, Czechoslovakia, and the former East Germany especially—is considerably higher than in the nineteen major industrial nations.

Light beer, introduced in 1974, accounts for 31 percent of the American beer market, more than in any other nation for which data is available. While Heineken, Beck's, Amstel Light, and Corona are popular in the United States, imports make up only 3 percent of our beer market.[21] In the spirits category, whiskey is the most consumed American drink (followed by vodka, gin, and rum), though it fell from 53 to 38 percent of the market between 1975 and 1987. Imports account for 37 percent of the spirits market and 17 percent of the wine market.

The legal drinking age in the United States, now 21 throughout the country, is the highest of any of the nineteen major industrial nations. European countries prohibit the sale of alcohol to persons under age 16 or 18 (or occasionally 20), though the laws are often not enforced.

Annual alcohol, beer, and wine consumption per capita, in liters, 1987:[22]

COUNTRY	ALCOHOL	BEER	WINE
Spain	3.00	64.5	54.0
Finland	2.98	68.1	9.3
Canada	2.50	82.8	10.2
United States	**2.47**	**90.1**	**9.1**
France	2.30	38.9	75.1
Japan	2.30	43.8	12.5
Germany	2.24	144.3	25.8
Belgium	2.20	121.0	23.0
Netherlands	2.07	84.3	14.6
Switzerland	2.04	69.3	49.5
Sweden	1.96	51.6	11.9
United Kingdom	1.70	110.5	12.0
New Zealand	1.60	120.8	15.3
Austria	1.59	116.2	32.1
Denmark	1.52	125.2	20.4
Ireland	1.51	102.8	3.5
Norway	1.32	51.4	5.9
Australia	1.20	111.3	20.6
Italy	1.00	25.6	79.0

Source (for chart and text): Margo Sparrow et al., *Alcohol Beverage Taxation and Control Policies*, 7th ed. (Ottawa: Brewers Association of Canada, 1989).

MARITAL, PREMARITAL, AND EXTRAMARITAL SEX

- **We're Number One in thinking that good sex makes a good marriage.**

What matters most in a marriage? Love? Fidelity? Friendship? Money? Or sex? While Americans do not put sex first on the list of important ingredients for a marriage, we rate it higher than shared religious beliefs, agreement on politics, children, and even common tastes and interests. In fact, more Americans say a happy sexual relationship is a very important aspect of a successful marriage (75.6 percent) than do respondents from any of the other nineteen major industrial nations.

Percentage of population saying that a happy sexual relationship is very important to a successful marriage, 1981–83:

COUNTRY	SEX VERY IMPORTANT	COUNTRY	SEX VERY IMPORTANT
United States	**75.6**	Belgium	66.6
Canada	75.2	Norway	65.2
United Kingdom[23]	73.8	Denmark	60.6
France	71.9	Sweden	59.3
Italy	71.8	Spain	57.3
Netherlands	69.3	Germany	55.5
Australia	68.7	Japan	35.3
Ireland	68.6		

Source: World Values Survey.

• **We're Number One in percentage of young people who say premarital sex should be avoided.**

It may not hold true for the majority, but about one fifth of American young people say that premarital sex should be avoided under any circumstances; that's more young celibacy advocates than in any of the other nineteen major industrialized nations surveyed. Another 70 percent of young Americans say that premarital sex is all right only if the parties concerned are in love. Only one in nine (11 percent) approve of premarital sex even if the parties are not in love. French young people are not so puritanical: twice as many approve of casual affairs of the flesh.

Percentage of young people age 18 to 24 who say that premarital sex should be avoided under any circumstances, and percentage who say premarital sex is all right even if the parties are not in love, 1988–89:

COUNTRY	AVOID SEX	SEX OKAY WITHOUT LOVE
United States	**19**	**11**
Australia	12	21
Japan	9	5
United Kingdom	6	21
Sweden	6	20
Germany	4	15
France	3	23

Source: Survey Research Consultants International, *Index to International Public Opinion, 1988–89* (New York: Greenwood Press, 1990), p. 631.

• We're Number One in percentage of people who say extramarital affairs can NEVER be justified.

More than seven out of ten Americans say it is *never* justifiable for a married man or woman to have an affair, according to the most recent international survey of citizens' values. A larger percentage of Americans hold this belief than do respondents in the remainder of the nineteen major industrial nations. Yet almost one third of Americans say they have had extramarital affairs (31 percent), according to another survey. These flings last one year on average, and only 28 percent of the adulterers say they plan to stop having affairs soon.[24] True to their reputation, 65 percent of the French say that adultery is fair at least sometimes— the largest percentage by far of the major industrial nations surveyed. Denmark leads in saying it is *always* just for married people to have affairs.

Percentage of population saying that a married man or woman having an affair can never, sometimes, or always be justified, 1981–83:

COUNTRY	NEVER	SOMETIMES	ALWAYS
United States	**73.9**	**24.4**	**1.7**
Ireland	72.1	26.4	1.5
Norway	70.2	28.7	1.2
Finland	69.7	28.4	1.9
Spain	66.6	30.2	3.2
Canada	66.5	31.5	2.0
Sweden	65.3	33.1	1.7
United Kingdom[25]	64.5	34.3	1.2
Germany	64.4	32.7	2.9
Italy	62.9	31.3	5.7
Belgium	61.3	36.8	1.9
Australia	57.8	39.2	3.0
Netherlands	57.3	40.4	2.2
Japan	57.1	41.7	1.2
Denmark	56.8	35.0	8.2
France	35.0	60.4	4.6

Source: World Values Survey.

SPORTS

- **We're Number One in attendance at a single sporting event.**
- **We're Number One in participation in a single sporting event.**

Europe's Tour de France cycling race attracts 10 million fans over three weeks, but the nation with the largest attendance at a single sporting event is the United States, where the New York Marathon draws an estimated 2.5 million live spectators each fall. Likewise, we're Number One in participation in a single sporting event: an annual 7.6-mile race in San Francisco draws more than 100,000 runners.

Also, don't forget the ninety-six-day Women's International Bowling Congress Championship, which drew more than 77,000 bowlers to Nevada in 1988. On the other side of the Atlantic, Prague, Czechoslovakia, regularly hosts a gymnastics festival with about 180,000 participants, though a mere 14,000 participate at one time.[26]

- **We're Number One in highest-paid athletes.**

Nine of the twenty highest-paid athletes in the world are Americans. Boxer Evander Holyfield, the highest-paid athlete in the world, earned about as much money in 1991 as two thousand American manufacturing workers. Boxing, auto racing, tennis, and golf are the most represented sports among the top twenty. Monica Seles, the seventeen-year-old tennis wonder, earned $7.6 million in 1991.

Twenty highest-paid athletes, in millions of dollars, 1991:

NAME	COUNTRY	INCOME[27]
Evander Holyfield	U.S.	$60.5 million
Mike Tyson	U.S.	31.5
Michael Jordan	U.S.	16.0
George Foreman	U.S.	14.5
Ayrton Senna	Brazil	13.0
Alain Prost	France	11.0
Razor Ruddock	Jamaica	10.2
Arnold Palmer	U.S.	9.3
Nigel Mansell	United Kingdom	9.0
Jack Nicklaus	U.S.	8.5
Larry Bird	U.S.	7.9
Monica Seles	Yugoslavia	7.6
Joe Montana	U.S.	7.5
Stefan Edberg	Sweden	7.4
Greg Norman	Australia	7.4
Steffi Graf	Germany	7.3
Andre Agassi	U.S.	7.3
Boris Becker	Germany	7.2
Wayne Gretzky	Canada	7.0
Gerhard Berger	Austria	7.0

Source: *Forbes*, August 19, 1991.

• **We're Number One in golf courses.**

Dan Quayle can rest easy: our economy may be waning, but we're still Number One in golf courses. Vice-President Quayle, who denies rumors that he plays an average of three golf games per week, has his choice of more than twelve thousand American courses.[28] In terms of crowds, he could do worse in other countries. There are almost seven thousand golfers per course in Japan (talk about playing through!), compared to about fifteen hundred golfers per course in the United States. Uruguay, on the other hand, claims only five hundred golfers for its four courses. Perhaps the Vice-President should consider visiting Uruguay, where he can play golf unbothered, and once again brush up on his Latin.

Ten countries with the most golf courses, 1988:

COUNTRY	GOLF COURSES	COUNTRY	GOLF COURSES
United States	**12,278**	New Zealand	411
Japan	1,441	South Africa	391
England	1,300	Ireland	259
Canada	1,224	Germany	210
Scotland	481	Argentina	207

Source: *Golf Digest Almanac, 1988* (New York: Golf Digest, 1989), p. 629.

READING, WRITING, AND IGNORANCE

EDUCATION AND ACHIEVEMENT

In 1983, the U.S. government released *A Nation At Risk,* a highly influential report whose most quoted line was: "If an unfriendly foreign power had attempted to impose on America the mediocre educational performance that exists today, we might well have viewed it as an act of war."[1] The alarming rhetoric of *A Nation At Risk* was answered with more alarm and then sputtering inaction: politicians huffed, the media gasped, task forces and blue ribbon panels were commissioned, and a new round of hollow manifestos was released to cure everything from early childhood education to teacher training. With a few exceptions, not much was done. As a result, America is now one stage past "at risk": we are feeling the pain.

Our high school dropout rate ranges from 10.5 percent for whites to 27.9 percent for Hispanics.[2] By comparison, 94 percent of Japanese students and almost 100 percent of German students finish high school on time.[3] For Americans who stay in school, things are not much better. High student–teacher ratios, crumbling buildings, and insufficient materials make it nearly impossible for many of our students to learn. Teachers in the United States spend more time just trying to *control* their classes than do teachers in Japan, Germany, or the United Kingdom.[4]

The effects of a deteriorating educational system are already apparent. Twenty-seven million American adults are functionally illiterate, according to Laubach Literacy International.[5] They cannot read to their children, or understand street signs or job applications. An additional forty million adults have a difficult time reading newspapers, financial documents, and other complex material.

Education has traditionally been the method by which a nation's future is ensured. After the Soviet Union launched Sputnik in 1957, an increased emphasis on teaching math and science in the United States helped us stay competitive in the space race. In the 1960s and beyond, desegregation, busing, and affirmative action helped alleviate racial discrimination—not only in schools, but throughout society. Now, in its dilapidated state, American education appears to be more of an impediment than a safeguard of our collective fate.

SPENDING

- **We're Number One in private spending on education.**
- **We're Number 17 in public spending on education.**

America's current education malaise has led many reformers to question whether the United States is investing enough money to yield a strong return. Are we slipping because we are not spending enough? If we spend more, will education improve? These questions are well intentioned but wide of the mark. America's primary concern should not be how *much* we spend on education, but *how* we allocate the money we already spend. That's not because the former issue isn't important, but because the latter is the cause of so many of the problems that beset American education.

Including public and private spending, the United States spends about 7 percent of its gross domestic product (GDP) on education annually, or around $330 billion. By this measure, we do fairly well; only a few developed nations spend more overall relative to the size of their economies.[6] But as with health care expenditures, the spending comparisons change dramatically when we distinguish between public and private sources. The

United States is first in private spending on education among the nineteen major industrial nations, but only seventeenth in public spending as a percentage of GDP. The results also mirror those of health care spending: topflight resources are generally available to those who can afford to pay for them, and the rest of America scrapes by on a public contribution smaller than that of all but one of the nineteen major industrial nations for which data is available.

Is our high private spending on education justified? It amounts to 1.7 percent of our GDP, almost a quarter of our total spending on education. Yet only 14 percent of students at all levels attend private schools.[7] In addition, many educators are challenging the conventional wisdom that private schools always provide a better education than public schools. Surely, there are some private schools that are leaps and bounds ahead of America's public schools. But "the fact is that both private and public education are doing a disastrously bad job," says Albert Shanker, president of the American Federation of Teachers. "If we are serious about our students meeting world-class standards . . . private school choice is not the answer."[8] Shanker's assessment, based on mathematics scores that show that private and public schools are not far apart in achievement, is particularly relevant given the Bush administration's emphasis on "school choice," which would most likely increase the privatization of American education.

Regarding America's low public spending relative to other nations, the United States is even worse off than the numbers show because of the arcane and grossly inequitable system by which public education is funded in the United States. In this respect as well, our public education system resembles our public health system in that it leaves so many Americans "uninsured" and exposed. Spending per student varies greatly from one school district to another because public contributions are linked to property taxes in these different areas. States are supposed to compensate for differences in property value by giving additional monies to the poorer districts according to a formula that is designed to ensure that enough money is available to provide a minimal standard of education. But the numbers show that the equalization process is a sham. As Jonathan Kozol reports in his book *Savage Inequalities,* a wealthy suburb of New York City with high property values spends $15,000 per student annually, while the city itself spends $7,300 per student. Affluent Princeton, New Jersey, spends $7,700 per pupil while poverty-stricken Camden, New Jersey, spends less than half that, $3,500 per pupil. In Texas, some districts spend as much as $19,000 per pupil annually, compared to just $2,100 in the poorest districts.[9] Lawsuits have been initiated in many states to rectify these inequalities, and a few have been successful.

Spending on education from public and private sources (and total), as a percentage of GDP, 1987:[10]

COUNTRY	PUBLIC $ AS A % OF GDP	PRIVATE $ AS A % OF GDP	TOTAL $ AS A % OF GDP
Denmark	7.50	0.07	7.57
Sweden	7.19	—	—
Netherlands	6.99	0.34	7.33
Norway	6.82	0.17	6.99
Canada	6.53	0.59	7.12
Austria	5.91	—	—
Ireland	5.84	0.28	6.12
France	5.57	1.03	6.59
New Zealand	5.37	—	—
Finland	5.31	0.49	5.80
Australia	5.25	0.38	5.63
Belgium[11]	5.12	—	—
Switzerland	5.01	0.10	5.11
Japan	4.98	1.41	6.38
United Kingdom	4.97	—	—
Italy	4.96	—	—
United States[12]	**4.77**	**1.68**	**6.44**
Germany	4.24	0.17	4.41

Source: Organization for Economic Cooperation and Development, *Education in OECD Countries 1987–88* (Paris: OECD, 1990), p. 115. Note: Figures do not add up exactly due to rounding.

COMPULSORY EDUCATION

- **We're Number One in providing compulsory education.**
- **We're Number 18 in providing compulsory education that meets the demands of a competitive economy.**

The United States provides as many years of free, full-time compulsory education as any nation, and Americans attend school longer than do students in any other nation for which data is available. American adults age 25 and over have had 12.2 years of schooling on average, compared to 10.4 years in Japan and 8.8 years in Germany.[13] Yet business leaders rate America behind all but one of the nineteen major industrial nations in the ability of the compulsory education system to effectively meet the needs of today's global economy.[14] School systems in Japan (75.5) and Germany (75.2) get the best ratings, far ahead of the United States (47.6). The lesson to be learned is that quantity does not always guarantee quality.

We're Number One!

**Years of free, full-time compulsory education provided, 1989;
and average rating (on an ascending scale of 1–100) of the
effectiveness of the nation's compulsory education system in
meeting the demands of a competitive economy, according to
business executives in each country, 1991:**

COUNTRY	YEARS PROVIDED	RATING
Japan	9	75.5
Germany	10	75.2
Switzerland	9	74.1
Ireland	9	72.2
Austria	9	71.2
Finland	10	65.6
Denmark	9	65.4
Netherlands	11	64.6
Belgium[15]	10	64.4
Australia	9	60.2
Canada	9	58.2
Sweden	9	57.9
Italy	8	51.4
France	10	49.7
Spain	8	48.9
New Zealand	9	48.6
Norway	9	48.2
United States	**11**	**47.6**
United Kingdom	11	40.6

Sources: United Nations Development Programme, *Human Development Report 1991* (New York: Oxford University Press, 1991), p. 181; *World Competitiveness Report 1991*, published by IMD International, Lausanne, Switzerland, and World Economic Forum, Geneva, Switzerland, p. 338.

ENROLLMENT

• **We're Number 9 in early childhood education.**

Early childhood education is critically important to a child's development and essential for society at large. Children gain important social and intellectual skills that ensure that they are ready to learn when they reach primary school. Each dollar spent on preschool education saves almost five dollars in later spending on special education, welfare, and crime control, according to the Children's Defense Fund.[16] Despite the potential benefits, only 56 percent of American four-year-olds are enrolled in school; eight of the nineteen major industrial nations do better. In France, Belgium, and the Netherlands, virtually all four-year-olds are enrolled in preschool.

In the mid 1960s, Congress implemented the Head Start program to provide disadvantaged American preschoolers with an early boost. While Head Start's educational and social services have proven successful, only about one quarter of eligible children currently benefit from the program because it is severely underfunded. Congress has called for increased funding of Head Start so that all eligible three- and four-year-olds and some five-year-olds will be able to participate.[17] Even if the monies are appropriated, many middle-class children will continue to be deprived of preschool education because they are ineligible for Head Start and their parents cannot afford private programs.

Percentage of four-year-olds enrolled in preprimary programs, 1987–90:[18]

COUNTRY	PREPRIMARY ENROLLMENT	COUNTRY	PREPRIMARY ENROLLMENT
France	100.0	**United States**	**56.1**
Belgium	98.1	Japan	54.6
Netherlands	97.9	Ireland	52.1
Spain	90.6	Norway	44.1
Germany	71.6	Canada	41.4
New Zealand	72.8	Finland	19.6
United Kingdom	69.2	Switzerland	18.7
Austria	63.4		

Source: Organization for Economic Cooperation and Development, *Education in OECD Countries 1987–88* (Paris: OECD, 1990), p. 107.

- **We're Number 15 in days spent in school each year.**

To kids in America, summer means lazy, playful days with no homework, no teachers . . . the stuff of Huck Finn and the juvenile American dream. Well, it may not last for long. Education policymakers increasingly believe that one reason why Johnny can't read (or multiply or spell) as well as some of his counterparts abroad is because he attends school for fewer days each year than students in many nations. The American school year is 180 days long on average, compared to 210 days in Germany, 211 days in the Soviet Union, and 243 days in Japan.

America's summer break from school dates "back to a time when family labor was vital to the late-summer harvest," says a recent *Time* magazine article.[19] Now, as an ingrained part of American education, the summer break gives us the shortest school year of all countries (except Belgium) among nations for which data is available. Breaking with tradition, some American schools have experimented with school years as long as 220 days. The reasons have as much to do with inner-city survival as international competition. "This has nothing to do with competition with the Japanese and everything to do with urban reality," says a school board member about one experiment. "This is eight hours when the drug addicts can't get at these kids."[20]

Number of days in an average school year, 1991:

COUNTRY[21]	DAYS IN SCHOOL	COUNTRY	DAYS IN SCHOOL
Japan	243	Canada	191
Israel	216	Finland	190
Soviet Union	211	New Zealand	190
Germany	210	Nigeria	190
Netherlands	200	France	185
Thailand	200	Ireland	184
Hungary	192	**United States**	**180**
United Kingdom	192	Belgium	168

Source: Education Commission of the States' Information Clearinghouse, January 1991.

- **We're Number One in higher education enrollment.**

Many Americans believe that the United States has the best higher education system in the world. After all, more than 18 percent of Americans age 20 to 24 are enrolled full time in postsecondary education, the largest percentage of all nations for which data is available.[22] We have the most universities of any nation, the most graduate programs, and the largest libraries. But these indicators measure the *quantity,* not *quality,* of American higher education.

In most industrialized nations, just attending college or university is considered a feat of educational achievement. Students are admitted only after taking grueling exams that test their knowledge in a variety of subjects; those who don't make the grade turn to vocational training or the job market. For example, about a third as many students per capita are enrolled in higher education in the United Kingdom as in the United States because in the U.K. most students do not pass the difficult exams required for entrance. While the United States has the infamous SAT and other standardized tests, there has essentially been a place for everyone who wanted to attend—between two-year colleges, community colleges, and larger universities—since the opening of American higher education during the postwar period.[23] "About 95 percent of our high school graduates—private as well as public—would be unable to get into college in any other industrialized country," says Albert Shanker.[24] "In the U.S., by contrast," says one recent study of American competitiveness, "even Bart Simpson would be able to find a college to admit him."[25] In Japan or Germany, Bart the underachiever would be shut out.

Educational reformers have also argued recently that, because of a decline in standards in American secondary education, U.S. colleges and universities are now left to give students the skills and knowledge that high schools once provided. This argument makes sense, looking at the global picture. In Japan, half as many people go to college as in the United States, despite the fact that a *greater* percentage of Japanese students obtain the qualifications necessary to go on to postsecondary education.[26] The logical conclusion, supported by comparisons of test scores (see test scores on the following pages), is that the Japanese students leave high school better educated than their American counterparts. Most, in fact, are ready to enter the job market without a college degree. As a result, Japanese students who do attend university are engaged in more advanced work, while many Americans are merely catching up. A good share of American college students, in fact, graduate with the same knowledge as a Japanese high school graduate—or less. "An average eighth grader in Japan knows more mathematics than a graduate of a master of business administration program in the United States," says Richard Lamm, former governor of Colorado, and an "average seventeen-year-old American knows half as much math as an average Swedish seventeen-year-old."[27]

Percentage of population age 20 to 24 enrolled full time in institutions of higher education, 1986–90:

COUNTRY	HIGHER ED. ENROLLMENT	COUNTRY	HIGHER ED. ENROLLMENT
United States[28]	**18.5**	Greece	13.2
Canada	15.9	Australia	12.2
France	14.6	Switzerland	12.0
Belgium	14.1	Sweden	11.3
Germany	14.1	Finland	11.2
Denmark	13.9	New Zealand	6.9
Netherlands	13.8	United Kingdom	6.3
Norway	13.5	Ireland	4.6

Source: United Nations Development Programme, *Human Development Report 1991* (New York: Oxford University Press, 1991), p. 181.

TEACHERS

• **We're Last in rewarding our teachers.**

Education policymakers have recognized the importance of rewarding committed educators. Yet veteran American teachers make less money than veteran teachers in seven other nations surveyed relative to per capita gross domestic product (GDP). At the starting level, American teachers make less than teachers in all seven nations except Japan. Switzerland leads in salaries for both starting and veteran teachers; the maximum salary for a Swiss secondary teacher is about three times the nation's per capita GDP.

Low wages discourage talented American college students from entering teaching. Public school teachers in the United States start with a salary of $20,529 on average, while their counterparts make $32,304 in entry-level positions in engineering, $27,408 in accounting, and $27,828 in sales.[29] Recently, as improving education has become a national priority and teachers' salaries have increased, there has been renewed interest in teaching among young Americans. Still, we have a long way to go to catch up with teachers' salaries in other countries.

Ratio of average teacher salary to per capita gross domestic product (GDP), 1988–90:[30]

COUNTRY	MAXIMUM SALARY (RATIO TO PER CAPITA GDP)	STARTING SALARY (RATIO TO PER CAPITA GDP)
Switzerland	2.97	1.69
Austria	2.60	0.98
Canada	2.22	1.10
Japan	2.21	0.75
Germany	2.19	1.37
United Kingdom	2.05	0.95
Australia	1.60	1.09
United States	**1.58**	**0.94**

Source: American Federation of Teachers.

MATH AND SCIENCE

- **We're Number One in percentage of students who say they're good at math.**
- **We're Last in percentage of students who *are* good at math.**

Math is a priority for Americans—at least we say it is. Eighty-three percent of Americans, more than any other nation surveyed, say it is absolutely necessary to know something about mathematics in order to be a well-rounded person. In fact, Americans are four times as likely to say this as the Japanese (21 percent) and more than twice as likely as the Germans (36 percent).[31]

In addition, more American students say that they are good at math than do students from other nations surveyed. Sixty-eight percent of American thirteen-year-olds agree with the statement "I am good at mathematics," three times as many as in South Korea (23 percent), where the smallest percentage of students say this. What's particularly alarming (or amusing) about our students' confidence is that they perform *worse* than any other nation included in this survey, and the most modest students, the Koreans, perform the best. Researchers in Korea note that "it would be against their tradition of humility for many of their students to answer 'yes,' to the question 'Are you good at math?' "[32] But that humility clearly doesn't exist among American students—and as the scores show, we have reason to be humble.

The International Assessment of Educational Progress (the study mentioned above) finds the United States to be the only nation among six studied where students perform *below* the mean average. According to the IAEP study, 97 percent of American thirteen-year-olds can add and subtract; 78 percent can do simple math problems, like using a number line; 40 percent (about half as many as in Korea) can do two-step problems; 9 percent (less than one quarter as many as in Korea) understand measurement and geometry concepts; and only 1 percent can interpret data in more advanced math problems. A second international math study, conducted by the International Association for the Evaluation of Educational Achievement (IEA), also shows abysmal results for the United States.[33]

Percentage of thirteen-year-old students who agree with the statement "I am good at mathematics," and math proficiency on a scale ranging from 0 to 1,000, with 500 as the mean, 1988:

COUNTRY	SAY THEY'RE GOOD AT MATH	MATH SCORE
United States	**68**	**473.9**
Canada[34]	61	522.8
Spain	60	511.7
Ireland	49	504.3
United Kingdom	47	509.9
South Korea	23	567.8

Source: Educational Testing Service, A World of Differences: An International Assessment of Mathematics and Science (Princeton, N.J.: ETS, 1989), pp. 14, 24.

And we'll balance the budget by then, too.

"By the year 2000, U.S. students will be first in the world in science and mathematics achievement," says President Bush's National Goals for Education, developed with the fifty governors.[35] But even Secretary of Education Lamar Alexander is skeptical of the President's optimism. "If our aim is to be first in the world in math and science by the year 2000," says Alexander, "there is an enormous challenge ahead of us."[36] Indeed, the challenge is so enormous as to make one wonder whether the President and the nation's governors knew when they set their goals just how badly America fares in international math and science comparisons. Maybe they should just shoot for a balanced budget.

- **We're Number One in percentage of young adolescents who DON'T think science is useful in everyday life.**
- **We're Last in science proficiency among young adolescents.**

Is what students learn in science relevant to everyday life? Only half of American thirteen-year-olds say it is, the smallest percentage of students in six nations surveyed.[37] No wonder: American students also say they spend more time in science class *reading* their textbook and less time doing experiments than any other nation studied. Seventy percent say reading the text is a common activity, while less than 20 percent say doing experiments is common.[38]

Perhaps that explains why the United States performs so poorly in a study of science proficiency among fourteen-year-olds conducted by the International Association for the Evaluation of Educational Achievement. Out of seventeen nations tested, only the Philippines and Hong Kong perform more poorly than the United States. America is outperformed by all of the nineteen major industrial nations tested, as well as Hungary and Poland, while Thailand and Singapore tie us.

Average science test scores among fourteen-year-olds in seventeen countries, 1983–86:

COUNTRY	SCIENCE SCORE	COUNTRY	SCIENCE SCORE
Hungary	21.7	Australia	17.8
Japan	20.2	Italy	16.7
Netherlands	19.8	United Kingdom[40]	16.7
Canada[39]	18.6	Singapore	16.5
Finland	18.5	Thailand	16.5
Sweden	18.4	**United States**	**16.5**
Poland	18.1	Hong Kong	16.4
South Korea	18.1	Philippines	11.5
Norway	17.9		

Source: International Association for the Evaluation of Educational Achievement, *Science Achievement in Seventeen Countries, A Preliminary Report* (New York: Pergamon Press, 1988).

- **We're Number 29 in scientists and technicians per capita.**

Egad! The United States has won the most Nobel prizes in science, but twenty-eight nations (including fourteen of the nineteen major industrial nations) have more scientists and technicians per capita than we do,[41] The United States has only 55 scientists and technicians per 1,000 persons, about six times fewer than Japan, which has 317 per 1,000 people.[42] The average among industrial nations is 139 scientists and technicians per 1,000.[43]

It's not surprising that we have so few scientists per capita, since only 30 percent of our college and university graduates major in science. Though the United States graduates about three hundred thousand students annually with bachelor's degrees in natural and applied sciences, seventy-five countries (including Iran, Peru, Swaziland, Haiti, and Afghanistan) have a greater percentage of students graduating from postsecondary institutions with science degrees.[44]

Scientists and technicians per 1,000 people, 1980–88:

COUNTRY	SCIENTISTS PER 1,000	COUNTRY	SCIENTISTS PER 1,000
Japan	317	Czechoslovakia	130
Austria	268	Spain	130
Sweden	262	Soviet Union	128
Canada	257	Bulgaria	113
Hungary	251	Norway	103
Ireland	244	Venezuela	95
Netherlands	219	France	83
Switzerland	202	Italy	83
Hong Kong	200	Israel	82
Yugoslavia	192	Peru	76
Poland	168	Argentina	75
Greece	166	Denmark	63
Cyprus	158	Kuwait	63
Australia	157	**United States**	**55**
Germany	131	New Zealand	49

Source: United Nations Development Programme, *Human Development Report 1991* (New York: Oxford University Press, 1991), pp. 128, 174.

GEOGRAPHY

- **We're Number One in percentage of people who say it is absolutely necessary to be able to read a map.**
- **We're Number One in ignorance of geography among young people.**

Where is the equator? The nearest mountain range? The next highway exit with a rest room? Americans place great value on the ability to read a map, according to a poll conducted by Gallup for the National Geographic Society. We lead nine countries surveyed in percentage of adults saying that being able to read a map is an "absolutely necessary" skill (69 percent).[45] Map reading is more important to us than being able to write a business letter, or use a calculator or a personal computer. Ninety-five percent of Americans say that it is important for us to know at least as much geography as people in other countries.[46]

Yet despite our cartographic compulsion, Americans age 18 to 24 rank dead last in geographic knowledge among the nine countries surveyed. On average, young Americans are able to correctly identify about seven of the following sixteen places on a world map: Canada, Central America, Egypt, France, Italy, Japan, Mexico, the Pacific Ocean, the Persian Gulf, South Africa, Sweden, the United Kingdom, the United States, the Soviet Union, West Germany, and Vietnam. The most geographically knowledgeable young respondents, the Swedes, are able to locate about twelve of the sixteen places.

Results of the poll among other age groups show that our knowledge of geography is declining. Respondents age 55 and older scored the *best* comparatively of all U.S. age groups: they were fifth among nine countries in geographic prowess. Those age 35 to 44 and 45 to 54 were sixth; and Americans age 25 to 34 were seventh. In fact, the United States was the only country in which geographic knowledge among the oldest group of respondents was higher than that of the youngest. The face of the earth is becoming increasingly unrecognizable to Americans.

Mean number of correct answers (out of sixteen) in a geography test given in nine countries, 1988:

COUNTRY	CORRECT ANSWERS, AGE 18 TO 24	CORRECT ANSWERS, AGE 55 AND OVER
Sweden	11.9	10.3
Germany	11.2	10.9
Japan	9.5	7.9
Canada	9.3	8.7
Italy	9.3	5.5
France	9.2	8.8
United Kingdom	9.0	7.8
Mexico	8.2	5.7
United States	**6.9**	**8.4**

Source: The Gallup Organization, "Geography: An International Gallup Survey" (Princeton NJ: Gallup, 1988), p. 55.

The United States . . . of Sweden?

Even if we don't know much about world geography, at least we know about our own country. Right? Wrong. Less than half of those Americans surveyed know that our population is between 150 million and 300 million people. In five other nations, more respondents know the population of the United States than we do. Only a third of young Americans know the approximate population of the United States, less than in all but one of the nations surveyed. At the top, young Swedes are 44 percent more likely to know the number of inhabitants in the United States than are the American inhabitants of the same age.

Percentage of population age 18 to 24 who know that the American population is between 150 million and 300 million people, 1988:

COUNTRY	KNOW U.S. POPULATION	COUNTRY	KNOW U.S. POPULATION
Sweden	46	France	35
Mexico	46	**United States**	**32**
Canada	42	United Kingdom	32
Germany	42	Italy	25
Japan	41		

Source: The Gallup Organization, "Geography: An International Gallup Survey" (Princeton, N.J.: Gallup, 1988), p. 59.

• **We're Number One in percentage of people who DON'T think it's important to be able to speak a foreign language.**

While it is true that Americans can usually make do with just English on tourist jaunts, the ability to speak foreign languages is essential as we move toward a global economy and as the United States itself becomes more diverse. The fact that fewer Americans than respondents in other nations surveyed think it is important to speak a foreign language does not augur well. *¿Comprendes?*

Percentage of population saying it is "absolutely necessary" or "not too important" to be able to speak a foreign language, 1988:

COUNTRY	ABSOLUTELY NECESSARY	NOT TOO IMPORTANT
Mexico	59	8
France	51	9
Italy	45	7
Germany	35	14
Sweden	34	10
Japan	29	13
Canada	23	24
United Kingdom	16	34
United States	**15**	**34**

Source: The Gallup Organization, "Geography: An International Gallup Survey" (Princeton, N.J.: Gallup, 1988), p. 70.

WORK HABITS

- **We're Number One in percentage of students who say they watch five or more hours of television a day.**
- **We're Number One in percentage of students who say they don't do their homework.**

American students are falling behind in math and science not only because of problems in school, but because few have home environments that are conducive to hard work and thinking. As with other age groups, young students in the United States watch more television than their foreign counterparts. They are also most likely to not do their homework.

Percentage of thirteen-year-old students who say they watch five or more hours of television a day, and percentage who say they don't do their homework, 1988:

COUNTRY	WATCH 5+ HOURS OF TV DAILY	DON'T DO HOMEWORK
United States	**31**	**5**
United Kingdom	27	2
Canada[47]	19	3
Ireland	14	2
Spain	13	1
Korea	7	3

Source: Educational Testing Service, *A World of Differences: An International Assessment of Mathematics and Science* (Princeton, N.J.: ETS, 1989), pp. 55–57.

DEBT ON ARRIVAL

THE ECONOMY

America may still be a land of opportunity, but it is increasingly a land of contradiction. Seemingly incompatible facts define our current economic situation. We are rich and we are poor. We live in luxury and we are homeless. Fragmentation is the legacy of the economic policies of the 1980s. As the middle class shrinks, haves and have-nots in the United States grow further and further apart.

The gap between rich and poor is expanding in other major industrial nations as well, but neither as swiftly nor as widely as in the United States. The Japanese economy has grown at unprecedented rates, Germany thrives despite the financial hurdles caused by reunification, and Scandinavian nations continue to provide high social spending and little poverty. America emerges from this series of snapshots as a complex Number One, able to claim the high ground in some areas of prosperity, but forced to accept leadership in some embarrassingly grim categories.

WEALTH AND POVERTY

- **We're Number One in billionaires.**
- **We're Number One in children and elderly in poverty.**

The world's richest man is not an American, and we're only fourth in billionaires per capita, but it is painfully ironic that the United States has the most billionaires in the world *and* the largest percentage of children living in poverty of any of the nineteen major industrial nations for which data is available.

One in five American children and one in ten elderly persons live in poverty. (Also, 43.2 percent of black children and 35.5 percent of Hispanic children in America live below the poverty level.)[1] That makes us Number One in percentage of children and adults age 65 and over living in poverty among the countries included in the Luxembourg Income Study, the most comprehensive multinational income study conducted to date. The most notable omission from the study, Japan, has low poverty rates.[2]

At the other end of the income scale, we're Number One in billionaires, according to *Forbes* magazine's 1991 annual survey of the world's wealthiest people. America boasts nearly one hundred fortunes of at least $1 billion, more than twice the number in Japan or Germany. Hong Kong, Switzerland, and Germany have the most billionaires per capita, followed by the United States. While Japan is home to the world's two richest men, Yoshiaki Tsutsumi and Taikichiro Mori (each worth about $15 billion), the United States edges out Japan in billionaire fortunes per capita. Sam Walton's $22 billion Wal-Mart fortune, the largest in America, is distributed among his family members. John Werner Kluge, with $5.9 billion, is the richest individual American. There were ninety-six American fortunes worth $1 billion or more in 1991 (sixty-four individuals and thirty-two families), down from ninety-nine in 1990.

Percentage of children and elderly living in poverty 1984–1987:[3]

COUNTRY	CHILDREN IN POVERTY	ELDERLY IN POVERTY
United States	**20.4**	**10.9**
Canada	9.3	2.2
Australia	9.0	4.0
United Kingdom	7.4	5.2
France	4.6	4.5
Netherlands	3.8	3.4
Germany	2.8	2.8
Sweden	1.6	4.3

Source: Timothy M. Smeeding, "U.S. Poverty and Income Security Policy in a Cross National Perspective," October, 1991, Luxembourg Income Study, working paper 70.

Number of individual and family fortunes worth $1 billion or more, and billionaire fortunes per 10 million population, 1991:

COUNTRY	BILLIONAIRES	PER 10 MILLION PEOPLE
United States	**96**	**3.8**
Japan	41	3.3
Germany (unified)[4]	40	5.1
Canada	9	3.4
France	9	1.6
Hong Kong	7	12.2
Italy	6	1.0
Switzerland	6	9.0
Saudi Arabia	6	3.5
United Kingdom	6	1.0
Taiwan	5	2.4

Sources (for chart and text): *Forbes*, July 23, 1990, July 22, 1991, and October 21, 1991.

Playing by capitalism's rules.

Throughout the world, 274 individuals or families worth at least $1 billion are identified on the *Forbes* 1991 list, with recent additions from Thailand and the Philippines. The total number of billionaires may actually be higher because the magazine does not include royal families, heads of state, and "dictators like Fidel Castro, because their wealth depends on police state repression, not on economic prowess."[5] Drug running apparently counts as "economic prowess," because the *Forbes* list includes two billion-plus Colombian cocaine fortunes whose kingpins are now behind bars. If only Fidel could learn to play fair like the drug lords.

- **We're Number One in real wealth.**
- **We're Number One in unequal wealth distribution.**

We are, in practical terms, the wealthiest nation on earth. In absolute terms, our economy is the largest, about $2 trillion larger in annual output than Japan's. Though five countries have a higher gross national product (GNP) per capita, the United States has the highest real gross domestic product (GDP) per capita, a better indicator of prosperity (an explanation is provided in the endnotes).[6]

While we're Number One in real wealth, we're also Number One (along with Australia and New Zealand) in unequal wealth distribution. The poorest 20 percent of the population in the United States receive less than 5 percent of all household income. The poorest 40 percent receive less than 20 percent, while the wealthiest 20 percent receive more than 40 percent of household income. In simple terms, the wealthiest fifth of America earns about nine times that of the poorest fifth. The poor and middle classes do better in Germany, Sweden, Japan, and Belgium, where wealth is distributed most equally.

Real gross domestic product (GDP) per capita and gross national product (GNP) per capita, 1989:

COUNTRY	REAL GDP PER CAPITA	GNP PER CAPITA
United States	**$20,690**	**$20,910**
Canada	19,230	19,030
Switzerland[7]	17,696	29,880
Norway	17,280	22,290
Japan	15,710	23,810
Sweden	15,670	21,570
Finland	15,230	22,120
Germany	15,220	20,440
France	14,480	17,820
Denmark	14,340	20,450
Australia	14,290	14,360
United Kingdom	14,070	14,610
Italy	13,920	15,120
Austria	13,710	17,300
Belgium	13,680	16,220
Netherlands	13,630	15,920
New Zealand	11,780	12,070
Spain	10,600	9,330
Ireland	8,540	8,710

Source: The World Bank, *World Development Report 1991* (New York: Oxford University Press, 1991), pp. 205, 263.

Percentage share of household income held by the poorest 40 percent of the population, 1979–87:

COUNTRY	PERCENT SHARE	COUNTRY	PERCENT SHARE
Belgium	22	Canada	18
Japan	22	Finland	18
Sweden	21	France	18
Germany	20	Denmark	17
Ireland	20	Switzerland	17
Netherlands	20	United Kingdom	17
Italy	19	Australia	16
Norway	19	New Zealand	16
Spain	19	**United States**	**16**

Sources (for chart and text): UNICEF, *The State of the World's Children 1991* (New York: Oxford University Press, 1991), p. 103; The World Bank, *World Development Report 1991* (New York: Oxford University Press, 1991), p. 263.

A serious gap.

Americans are concerned about the inequality of wealth distribution in the United States. When told that "over the past ten years, the income of the poorest 20 percent of the families in the U.S. has gone down 9 percent, while the income of the richest 20 percent has gone up 19 percent," nine out of ten Americans respond that this is a serious problem. Seven out of ten say it is very serious.

Source: The Harris Poll, April 15, 1990.

- **We're Number One in big homes.**
- **We're Number One in homelessness.**

The United States leads the nineteen major industrial nations in homelessness and in percentage of people living in big homes, homes with five or more rooms. (We're also Number 3 in home ownership, behind only Finland and Australia).[8] Is there a contradiction in these statistics? In poverty-stricken areas, big homes may be crowded. But in the average American household, 2.3

people live in 5.4 rooms. With more than two rooms per person, that's ample space, and almost one in seven homes has eight rooms or more.[9]

Counting homeless persons is a difficult task throughout the world. Estimates vary depending on who's doing the counting: the government, private organizations, or advocates for the homeless. Usually, governments report lower numbers and advocates report higher numbers of homeless persons. There are three million homeless people in the United States, according to the Coalition for the Homeless, a national advocacy group. The U.S. Department of Housing and Urban Development claims there are as many as 600,000 homeless persons, though the 1987 study from which this figure is derived also acknowledged that more than one million people might have been homeless for some period of the previous year.[10] Given that the government's homeless estimates doubled between 1983 and 1987, it is not unlikely that the Coalition for the Homeless's figure of three million homeless persons is correct as of 1992.[11] If so, there are as many homeless people in America as there are homeless in all of Western Europe, according to figures provided by the European Federation of National Organizations Working with the Homeless. The Belgium-based group estimates that 2.5 million of the 3 million homeless persons in Western Europe are members of families headed primarily by single women. The European Federation reports 600,000 homeless persons in Germany, 560,000 in the United Kingdom, 400,000 in France, 260,000 in Spain, 25,000 in Portugal, 50,000 in the Netherlands, 20,000 in Denmark, 20,000 in Belgium, and 5,000 in Ireland. There are an estimated 100,000 homeless persons in Canada.[12]

Homelessness may be ubiquitous in America, but certain groups have felt a disproportionate amount of the pain. Forty-six percent of the homeless are black and 15 percent are Hispanic, according to a December 1990 study by The U.S. Conference of Mayors that surveyed the homeless population in thirty major American cities; 34 percent are white, and 4 percent are of other ethnic backgrounds.[13] By contrast, 12 percent of the overall U.S. population is black and 8 percent is Hispanic.[14] Fifty-one percent of the homeless are single men, according to the study, and 34 percent are families with children; more than a quarter are mentally ill and nearly four in ten have substance abuse problems. One quarter of homeless people are war veterans.

Percentage of homes with five or more rooms, and percentage of homes with one room only, 1980–89:

COUNTRY	FIVE OR MORE ROOMS (%)	ONE ROOM (%)
United States	**70.3**	**0.8**
Ireland	57.9	2.4
Germany	36.4	2.4
Norway	36.0	5.0
France	35.9	9.1
Belgium	35.6	1.0
Italy	34.6	1.7
Denmark	27.6	5.1
United Kingdom	25.1	9.1
Switzerland	24.0	8.5
Spain	23.5	11.5
Austria	22.0	7.0
Sweden	21.4	13.0
Finland	12.1	17.3
Netherlands	8.2	5.9

Sources (for chart and text): *American Housing Survey for the United States in 1989* (Washington, D.C.: USGPO, 1991), pp. 38–50; *European Marketing Data and Statistics 1991* (London: Euromonitor Publications, 1991), p. 360.

A toilet of one's own.

Toilets are taken for granted in the United States and other developed countries. But 155,000 American households have no flush toilet at all and more than two million American households are forced to share facilities with others. Breakdowns are a serious problem as well. Five million American households reported having no operable toilet in their home within the last three months.

SPENDING, SAVING, AND DEBT

- **We're Number One in defense spending.**
- **We're Last in spending on the poor, the aged, and the disabled.**

A no-nonsense statesman once said, "To wage war, you need first of all money; second, you need money; and third, you also need money."[15] Funds spent in one place are funds lost in another. Critics of the U.S. military buildup of the 1980s argued that unchecked defense spending would severely hamper our nation's well-being in other areas. The effects are now apparent: the United States is Number One in defense spending among the nineteen major industrial nations, but Number 17 in public spending on education, Number 13 in public spending on health care, and last in spending on the poor, the aged, and the disabled.

About 30 percent of U.S. federal government expenditures go to housing, social security, welfare, and related programs. These funds provide low-income housing; community development and improvement; sanitary services; disability and unemployment payments; and welfare for the aged, the disabled, and children. Sweden and Switzerland spend the most (more than 50 percent of their central government spending) on these vital concerns.

In relative terms, the United States spends twice as much on defense as the next-biggest military spender, the United Kingdom—this despite the fact that our defense spending has decreased from 1972, when it made up almost a third of the government's budget (32.2 percent). Fifty percent of Americans think we spend too much on defense, 36 percent think we spend the "right amount," and 9 percent think we spend too little, according to a Gallup poll.[16]

Relative to government expenditures, spending on the poor, the aged and the disabled fell by 20 percent between 1983 and 1989, while military spending rose 4 percent. As communism becomes confined to history books, the majority of American politicians and military officials agree that at least some of the money appropriated for the military could be better spent elsewhere. The administration's defense budget request for fiscal year 1991 represented the first reduction in real terms (albeit small: 2.6 percent) since the Vietnam War.[17] Disputes will continue as to how much the defense budget can be substantially cut, but in the end it is likely that the United States will stay Number One in military spending. The pivotal question will remain: At what cost?

Percentage of central government expenditures spent on housing, social security, welfare, and related programs; and percentage spent on defense, 1987–89:[18]

COUNTRY	HOUSING, SOCIAL SECURITY, WELFARE	DEFENSE
Sweden	55.9	6.5
Switzerland	50.6	10.3
Germany	49.4	8.7
Austria	48.3	2.7
Belgium	43.9	4.7
France	40.7	6.1
Netherlands	40.6	5.0
Norway	39.6	7.8
Italy	38.6	3.6
Denmark	37.8	5.4
Canada	37.0	7.3
Spain	37.0	6.5
Finland	36.5	5.1
United Kingdom	34.0	12.5
New Zealand	33.8	4.8
Ireland	30.3	2.8
Japan	30.3	6.5
Australia	29.3	8.9
United States	**29.3**	**24.6**

Sources (for chart and text): The World Bank, *World Development Report 1991* (New York: Oxford University Press, 1991), p. 225; International Monetary Fund, *Government Finance Statistics Yearbook 1990* (Washington, D.C.: IMF, 1990), pp. 58–63.

- **We're Number One in spending our R&D funds on defense.**

While Japan and Germany commit almost all of their research and development funds to improving industry, agriculture, technology, and education—areas that have ensured their competitiveness internationally—the United States is busy fueling its military machine. Defense-related R&D makes up 65 percent of our total government R&D spending, a larger percentage than that of any of the nineteen major industrial nations. In relative terms, we spend nearly twenty times as much on defense research as Japan and five times as much as Germany. As our slippage in industry, education, environmental control, and other areas makes painfully clear, the money that drives our brain power is needed elsewhere.

Percentage of government research and development funds spent on defense, 1989:

COUNTRY	PERCENTAGE OF R&D SPENT ON DEFENSE[19]	COUNTRY	PERCENTAGE OF R&D SPENT ON DEFENSE
United States	**65.4**	Norway	6.8
United Kingdom	45.5	Japan	3.5
France	37.0	Netherlands	3.2
Sweden	24.1	New Zealand	2.5
Spain	19.1	Finland	1.6
Switzerland	17.1	Belgium[20]	0.6
Germany	12.8	Denmark	0.4
Italy	10.3	Austria	0.1
Australia	9.0	Ireland	0.0
Canada	7.9		

Source: *World Competitiveness Report 1991*, published by IMD International, Lausanne, Switzerland, and World Economic Forum, Geneva, Switzerland, p. 322. Original: OECD, *Main Science and Technology Indicators, 1990* (Paris: OECD, 1990).

- **We're Number One in military aid to developing countries.**
- **We're Last in humanitarian aid to developing countries.**

Our priorities here are crystal clear. The United States is Number One in military aid, but last in humanitarian aid to developing countries. America leads the world in arms transfers to Third World countries, yet we commit the smallest percentage of our GNP to development aid of any of the nineteen major industrial nations.[21]

Until recently, the former Soviet Union had a substantial lead over the United States in arms transfers to developing nations. However, because of the Soviet Union's retreat from the arms market and the aftermath of the Persian Gulf war, the United States has become Number One in dealing deadly weapons to the Third World. An arms order from Saudi Arabia worth $14.5 billion pushed the total value of U.S. transfers to the Third World from $8 billion in 1989 to $18.5 billion in 1990.[22] Meanwhile the USSR's share of the Third World market dropped for the third year in a row down to 29 percent. The United States now holds 45 percent of the market.

In absolute terms, $7.68 billion worth of U.S. development aid may seem substantial, but France gives almost as much ($7.45 billion),[23] and Japan gives substantially more ($8.95 billion).[24] In relative terms, only .15 percent (less than one sixth of 1 percent) of our GNP goes to official development assistance for poor countries. Of that tiny percentage, only 13 percent goes to the world's poorest nations, those defined by the U.N. as least developed countries (LDCs). Norway gives seven times as much aid as does the United States in relative terms, three times as much to LDCs. Canada and Germany contribute almost three times as much, Japan and the U.K. more than twice as much, and they give a larger share to the nations that need it most. Despite our meager giving, Americans by a four-to-one margin think the United States spends too much on official development aid, and half of those polled oppose economic aid to foreign countries altogether.[25]

Arms transfer agreements with the Third World, expressed as a percentage of total, 1989 and 1990:

COUNTRY	1989 (%)	1990 (%)
United States	**23.6**	**44.8**
Soviet Union	38.5	29.2
China	4.3	6.3
France	11.0	5.5
Other European nations	6.0	5.4
All others	5.3	4.0
United Kingdom	8.0	3.8
Italy	0.8	0.6
Germany	2.6	0.5

Source: Richard F. Grimmett, "Conventional Arms Transfers to the Third World, 1983–1990," August 2, 1991, a Congressional Research Service report to Congress, p. 47.

Total official development aid as a percentage of gross national product, and percentage of aid going to least developed countries (LDCs), 1989:

COUNTRY	DEVELOPMENT AID (% OF GNP)	PERCENT FOR LDCS
Norway	1.04	39
Sweden	.97	30
Denmark	.94	42
Netherlands	.94	30
France[26]	.70	20
Finland	.63	48
Belgium	.46	30
Canada	.44	37
Italy	.42	35
Germany	.41	27
Australia	.38	23
Japan	.32	18
United Kingdom	.31	33
Switzerland	.30	36
Austria	.23	22
New Zealand	.22	12
Ireland	.17	38
United States	**.15**	**13**

Source: United Nations Development Programme, *Human Development Report* (New York: Oxford University Press, 1991), p. 187.

• We're Number 6 in private philanthropy for developing countries.

Like the U.S. government, the American people are far less forthcoming with charity than their counterparts in other nations. While we're Number One in real wealth and private consumption, we're only Number 6 in philanthropic donations to developing nations in per capita terms. The Scandinavian countries, Switzerland, and Germany give the most per capita, with Sweden contributing fourteen dollars per person, five dollars more than the average American. The Italians seem particularly cheap, given their means: they give less than fifty cents per head privately.

Private voluntary aid to developing countries per capita, 1988:

COUNTRY	PRIVATE AID PER CAPITA	COUNTRY	PRIVATE AID PER CAPITA
Sweden	$14.00	United Kingdom	4.00
Norway	13.00	Australia	3.00
Switzerland	13.00	Austria	3.00
Netherlands	12.00	Finland	3.00
Germany	11.00	France	2.00
United States	**9.00**	New Zealand	2.00
Canada	8.00	Belgium	1.00
Ireland	6.00	Japan	1.00
Denmark	4.00	Italy	< .50

Source: U.S. Bureau of the Census, *Statistical Abstract of the United States 1991* (Washington, D.C.: USGPO, 1991), p. 863. Original: Organization for Economic Cooperation and Development (Paris), unpublished data.

- **We're Number One in private consumption.**
- **We're Last in investing and saving.**

Investing and saving are two smart things to do with money. Unfortunately, we like to spend more than we like to invest or save. In fact, consumer spending accounts for more of our gross domestic product (GDP) than that of any of the nineteen major industrial countries. And our gross domestic investment and gross domestic savings rates are lower than that of any of the nineteen major industrial countries.[27] This doesn't bode well for the economic stability of the United States. As a report of the Council on Competitiveness says: "America's low investment rate impairs both productivity and income growth . . . [areas in which we have] lagged behind other industrial countries over the past two decades."[28]

By not investing, we allow foreign investors to sink their money into our real estate and businesses. If we don't start saving, we're going to need a lot more help from foreign creditors as the baby boomers hit old age and come to rely on Social Security and Medicare. Our track record in these areas is getting worse, not better. From 1979 to 1989, American domestic savings decreased from 21 to 13 percent of GDP. During the same period, Germany and Japan upped their savings rates; they now save twice as much as the United States in relative terms.[29] Our profligacy may also make us Number One in personal bankruptcy. More than 700,000 Americans—about one in 250 adults—declared bankruptcy in 1990, an increase of 16 percent over the previous year.[30]

Apparently, America's attitude toward spending and saving changed during the last two decades. A 1973 poll conducted by Gallup International found Americans age 18 to 24—the core of today's spenders—to be more frugal than their foreign counterparts. Compared to their contemporaries in France, Germany, Japan, Sweden, Switzerland, and the United Kingdom, the Americans were most likely to *disagree* with the statement "money is for spending, not saving."[31]

Private consumption spending as a percentage of GDP and in real dollars per capita, 1989:

COUNTRY	PRIVATE CONSUMPTION (% OF GDP)	PRIVATE CONSUMPTION PER CAPITA
United States	**67**	**$13,900**
United Kingdom	64	9,200
Belgium	63	8,500
Spain	63	6,400
Italy	62	8,600
France	60	8,800
Netherlands	60	8,200
Australia	59	8,400
Canada	59	11,400
Switzerland	58	10,300
Japan	57	8,800
New Zealand	58	7,100
Ireland	57	5,100
Austria	55	7,500
Finland	54	7,800
Germany	54	8,200
Denmark	53	7,600
Sweden	52	8,100
Norway	48	8,400

Source: The World Bank, *World Development Report 1991* (New York: Oxford University Press, 1991), p. 221; Organization for Economic Cooperation and Development, *Environmental Indicators* (Paris: OECD, 1991), p. 63.

Gross domestic investment and savings as a percentage of GDP, 1989:

COUNTRY	DOMESTIC INVESTMENT AS A % OF GDP	DOMESTIC SAVINGS AS A % OF GDP
Japan	33	34
New Zealand	32	28
Finland	30	28
Switzerland	30	29
Austria	27	28
Norway	27	32
Australia	26	23
Spain	25	22
Italy	24	23
Canada	23	23
Germany	22	27
Sweden	22	22
France	21	22
Ireland	21	29
United Kingdom	21	18
Belgium	20	22
Denmark	19	23
Netherlands	19	23
United States	**15**	**13**

Source: The World Bank, *World Development Report 1991* (New York: Oxford University Press, 1991), p. 221.

- **We're Number One in credit cards and ATM machines.**

Contributing to American financial troubles is the fact that we're Number One in credit card ownership and automated teller machines (ATMs). Approximately 1.3 billion credit cards are currently in circulation in the United States, including 220 million Visa and Mastercards and 1.1 billion cards issued by American Express, Sears, and various merchants. Eighty percent of American adults have either a bank, retail, or gas card, and many Americans have seven or more cards. About 150 million ATM cards have been issued to Americans and we now have more than 75,000 ATMs at our disposal, seven times as many as in the U.K. and twenty times as many as in Germany. The active ATM user visits a machine more than once a week; the average withdrawal is more than $67. Combined with credit card interest rates aproaching 20 percent, it's no wonder we can't save!

Sources: Europe: *European Marketing Data and Statistics 1991* (London: Euromonitor Publications, 1991), p. 165; U.S.: Michael Quint, "Banks Uneasy at Focus on Credit Cards," *The New York Times*, November 19, 1991, p. A1; Bankcard Holders of America. Original: Nilson.

- **We're Number One in budget deficit.**
- **We're Number One in foreign debt.**
- **We're Number One in innumeracy.**

Could our government's monetary problems be related to our society's lack of proficiency with numbers? Innumeracy is "an inability to deal comfortably with the fundamental notions of numbers and chance," according to mathematician and author John Allen Paulos.[32] The pervasiveness of innumeracy in our society, Paulos argues, gravely affects the decisions we make and our general understanding of the world.

Perhaps it's no coincidence, then, that our students score last in international mathematics tests (see Math and Science in the previous chapter) *and* we have the most foreign debt and the largest budget deficit of any nation in the world. Lessons learned (or not learned) in childhood stay with us throughout life. For example, thirteen-year-olds in different countries were asked whether they thought math was useful in solving everyday problems—like budgets. Fewer of the American students thought that mathematics was applicable to "real life" than did the students in other countries.[33]

What if the world's leaders were asked the same question—Mr. President, do you believe math is useful in solving government's budget problems? In alleviating our status as the world's largest debtor nation? Based on our inability to control the growth of foreign debt and the budget deficit, the United States again appears to be Number One in divorcing mathematics from reality. The Congressional Budget Office projects that the U.S. budget deficit will increase from $279 billion in 1991 to $362 billion in 1992.[34] These estimates include $77 billion in 1991 and $115 billion in 1992 for the bailout of the savings and loan industry and other insolvent banks insured by the federal government. The 1991 deficit estimate is also misleadingly low because it includes a one-time credit of $48 billion from our Desert Storm allies. While our budget deficit is the largest in the world in absolute terms, our deficit is not nearly as sizable as that of Italy or Ireland relative to gross domestic product.

Our foreign debt is approaching $400 billion, a substantial portion of our $2.2 trillion debt overall. Germany has the second largest foreign debt, close to $100 billion. In relative terms, the U.S. foreign debt is equivalent to 7.5 percent of GDP, twenty-five times as much as Japan's foreign debt, which is only 0.3 percent of their GDP. A number of small nations, including Ireland, Belgium, Denmark, and New Zealand, have much higher foreign debt than the United States relative to the size of their economies.[35]

**Budget surpluses and deficits of the nineteen major industrial
nations, 1989–91:**[36]

COUNTRY	SURPLUS/DEFICIT ($ BILLION)	AS % OF GDP
United States	**−279.0**	**−5.0**
Italy	−97.5	−11.3
Japan	−51.1	−1.8
France	−17.8	−1.9
Canada	−15.4	−2.8
Spain	−11.4	−3.9
Belgium	−11.0	−6.8
Netherlands	−9.9	−4.4
Austria	−5.1	−4.0
Ireland	−2.9	−9.7
Norway	−1.0	−1.0
Switzerland	−1.0	−0.6
Germany	−0.9	−0.1
Australia	+1.1	+0.5
Finland	+2.3	+2.0
New Zealand	+3.0	+7.2
Denmark	+4.1	+4.0
Sweden	+7.5	+4.0
United Kingdom	+10.4	+1.3

Sources (for chart and text): International Monetary Fund, *Government Finance Statistics Yearbook 1990*
(Washington, D.C.: IMF, 1990), p. 78; *World Competitiveness Report 1991*, published by IMD Interna-
tional, Lausanne, Switzerland, and World Economic Forum, Geneva, Switzerland, p. 250; Congressional
Budget Office, *The Economic and Budget Outlook: An Update*, August 1991.

TRADE

• **We're Number One in trade stagnation.**

America's trade deficit was $101 billion (or about $400 per
person) in 1990, the most recent year for which data is available.
In recent years, particularly in 1991, our trade balance has improved. Still, one reason our trade deficit is so large is because
during the 1980s we led the nineteen major industrial countries in stagnation of exports, and we were a close second for
increasing reliance on imports. While American exports are now

growing at a strong pace, between 1980 and 1989 our average annual growth rate for exports (2.3 percent) was about half that of other industrial nations, and our import growth rate (8.2 percent) was about double that of other nations. In other words, we became increasingly dependent on other nations, while they became less dependent on us. A shining example of our loss of trade power can be seen in the fact that, though we have more than three times Germany's population, their exports to major industrial nations were worth $50 billion more than ours in 1989.

Our trade deficit has been reduced from its high of $152 billion in 1987. But deficits with key trading partners continue. The Council on Competitiveness notes that in 1989, two thirds of our trade imbalance was with Japan and the "Four Tigers": Taiwan, Hong Kong, Singapore, and South Korea. In 1990, our trade deficit with Japan alone was $41 billion, twice what it was in 1983, though not as high as in 1987 when the imbalance was just shy of $60 billion. American imports of cars and trucks, telecommunications equipment, and consumer electronics constitute the great majority of our trade deficit with Japan, which has the largest trade surplus in the world—it may reach $100 billion in 1992.[37]

Average annual growth rate of exports, percent, 1980 to 1989:

COUNTRY	AVERAGE GROWTH (%)	COUNTRY	AVERAGE GROWTH (%)
Ireland	7.4	Germany	4.4
Spain	7.4	Australia	4.1
Norway	6.8	Switzerland	3.8
Canada	6.0	Italy	3.7
Denmark	5.3	New Zealand	3.5
Austria	5.1	France	3.3
Sweden	4.9	Finland	3.2
Belgium	4.7	United Kingdom	2.7
Japan	4.6	**United States**	**2.3**
Netherlands	4.5		

Source: The World Bank, World Development Report 1991 (New York: Oxford University Press, 1991), p. 231.

• **We're Number One in tobacco exports.**

A double standard is apparent in the trade policies of the United States regarding products that are harmful to the human body. If we are vigilant in our attempts to stem the flow of cocaine and other drugs into this country—and we should be—why do we turn the other way when the substance being traded is tobacco? America leads the world in tobacco exports, with 219,000 tons exported in 1988. Tobacco is obviously different than most narcotics; after all, it's legal, it takes longer to kill, and it doesn't drive citizens to steal in order to get a fix. But the U.S. Surgeon General's figures show that two hundred times as many Americans die each year from smoking as from cocaine abuse. Smoking is "by far the leading cause of premature mortality in developed countries," says the World Health Organization.[38]

Source: *The Economist World Book of Vital Statistics* (New York: Times Books, 1990), p. 96.

• **We're Number One in being trusted by the Japanese.**
• **Japan is Number 11 in being trusted by us.**

Discussion of trade policy in the United States often deteriorates into Japan bashing, as free-market advocates lament Japan's unwillingness to fully eliminate barriers to foreign imports. Coupled with Japanese acquisitions of Rockefeller Center, American film and music companies, and other "apple pie" U.S. institutions, resentment has surfaced among some Americans.

When asked, "What countries do you think can be trusted?" the Japanese answer unequivocally: the United States. The trust, however, is not reciprocal. Americans trust ten nations more than they trust Japan, according to a 1989 poll. Fifty-four percent of the Japanese respondents say they trust the United States, while only 15 percent of the American respondents say they trust Japan. The top pick of the Americans is our northern neighbor, Canada, with an impressive 73 percent of respondents deeming them trustworthy. Overall, the United Kingdom is the most trusted nation, coming in second in both polls. Australia is uniformly third.

Seventy percent of the Japanese population, according to a separate 1991 poll, say they think Americans look down on the Japanese—an interesting fact in light of a Japanese legislative leader's controversial claim that Americans are "lazy" and a third of them "cannot even read." Three quarters of the Japanese also say the United States is blaming Japan for its own economic problems.[39]

Top fifteen answers of Japanese and U.S. citizens to the question, "What countries do you think can be trusted?", 1989:

JAPAN	PERCENT	UNITED STATES	PERCENT
United States	54	Canada	73
United Kingdom	51	United Kingdom	52
Australia	35	Australia	48
France	33	Switzerland	41
Switzerland	31	Sweden	37
Canada	30	France	33
West Germany	29	West Germany	23
Netherlands	12	Norway	23
Sweden	10	New Zealand	19
Italy	10	Italy	17
China	9	Japan	15
Brazil	7	Netherlands	15
South Korea	6	Mexico	13
Singapore	4	Israel	11
Norway	3	Poland	7

Source: Survey Research Consultants International, *Index to International Public Opinion 1989–90* (New York: Greenwood, 1991), pp. 684–85.

FINANCE

- **We're Number One in Fortune 500 international companies.**
- **We're Number One in Fortune 500 international companies that lose money.**

The United States' shining star, General Motors, is also its prodigal son. With $125 billion in annual sales, GM is the largest company in the world, but it posted a $2 billion loss in 1990.[40] Twelve other U.S. companies on *Fortune*'s international list of the five hundred largest companies also ended 1990 with negative balances.

The United States has the most companies, 164, on the *Fortune* Global 500, but, per capita, Japan has more and Sweden has more than three times as many.

Number of companies on the *Fortune* Global 500 list of the largest industrial companies in the world, top ten countries; and number of companies on the list from these countries that lost money in the previous year, 1990:

COUNTRY	NUMBER	LOST MONEY
United States	**164**	**13**
Japan	111	1
Britain	43	1
France	30	4
Germany	30	2
Sweden	17	1
Canada	12	2
South Korea	11	0
Switzerland	11	1
Australia	9	2

Source: *Fortune*, July 29, 1991.

- **We're Number One in bankers.**
- **We're Number One in poor bank performance.**
- **We're Number One in bank failures and bailouts.**

A 1991 survey of major banks in the seven biggest banking nations in the world finds Japan first in profitability and the United States last. The study by the Federal Reserve Bank of New York charts the relative performance, between 1985 and 1989, of fifty-one internationally active financial institutions in Canada, France, Germany, Japan, Switzerland, the United Kingdom, and the United States. By conventional measures, the U.S. banks perform horrendously.

In two categories of profitability—real return on equity and real return on assets—we are seventh out of seven nations. Japan is first in the former category, second in the latter. The United States also places last in real revenue growth and sixth in real asset growth. Japan is first in both growth categories. Only one American bank makes the top ten in total assets. Japan has six banks in the top ten. Our banks are average in productivity and capitalization. Japan is first in two of three categories.[41]

As if poor bank performance weren't bad enough, the United States is also undoubtedly Number One in bank failures and bailouts. At the fore, of course, is the savings and loan crisis, punishment in part for what seemed to be a borrow-now-pay-never mentality in the thrift industry. The bailout of the S&L's and other insolvent banks will cost the United States $77 billion in 1991 and $115 billion in 1992, according to estimates of the Congressional Budget Office.[42]

Despite our banking problems, the United States leads in percentage of labor force working in financial industries, including banking, real estate, and insurance. Nearly fourteen million Americans—more than one in ten of the work force—were employed in finance in 1989.

Commercial banks' profitability, measured by real return on equity, 1985 to 1989:[43]

COUNTRY	PERCENT RETURN	COUNTRY	PERCENT RETURN
Japan	11.5	United Kingdom	4.2
France	9.7	Canada	3.5
Germany	6.8	**United States**	**1.6**
Switzerland	5.3		

Source: The Federal Reserve Bank of New York, "International Competitiveness of U.S. Financial Firms," May 1991, pp. 13–15.

Percent of economically active population working in "financing, insurance, real estate and business services," 1986–89:

COUNTRY	PERCENT	COUNTRY	PERCENT
United States	**11.0**	Norway	7.4
Australia	10.9	Belgium	7.3
Switzerland	10.5	France	7.3
United Kingdom	9.4	Ireland	6.4
Netherlands	9.1	Germany	6.4
Sweden	8.2	Austria	5.9
Denmark	8.1	Canada	5.7
Japan	7.7	Spain	4.6
Finland	7.6	Italy	3.6

Source: International Labor Organization, *Yearbook of Labor Statistics 1989–90* (Geneva: ILO, 1990), pp. 46–119.

WORK AND PRODUCTIVITY

- **We're Number One in managers.**
- **We're Last in growth of industrial productivity.**

The United States has the most managers per employee, yet during the last decade our industrial output has grown the least of all the nineteen major industrial nations.[44] Is our managerial class overinflated and out of touch with the rank and file? Japan, a leader in growth of labor productivity, has three times *fewer* managers per employee than the United States. Finland, the top performer, experienced five times as much growth as the United States with one quarter the number of managers per employee. In fact, there seems to be an inverse relationship throughout between management size and productivity. Managers make up about 6.0 percent of the labor force on average in industrialized nations, compared to 12.1 percent in America. Growth of productivity between 1979 and 1990 was 2.0 percent on average in major European nations and 0.7 percent in the United States.

Percent of economically active population who are managers or administrative workers, 1989; and percentage average annual growth of labor productivity, in output per employee, 1979 to 1990:

COUNTRY	MANAGERS (%)[45]	PRODUCTIVITY GROWTH (%)
United States	**12.1**	**0.7**
Australia	11.9	0.9
Canada	11.9	1.2
Austria	4.7	1.9
Japan	3.7	3.0
Netherlands	3.3	1.5
Denmark	3.0	2.1
Finland	3.0	3.6
Ireland	2.2	—
Spain	1.3	3.0

Sources: International Labor Organization, *Yearbook of Labor Statistics 1989–90* (Geneva: ILO, 1990), pp. 120–186; Organization for Economic Cooperation and Development, *OECD Economic Outlook 50* (Paris: OECD, 1991), p. 136.

- **We're Number One in impact of substance abuse on the job.**

A survey of executives around the world ranks the United States last in long-term planning, eleventh in worker identification with the company, and first in impact of substance abuse in the workplace. It is probably not a coincidence that the Japanese lead in worker identification, are last in substance abuse on the job, and are Number One in productivity growth. Americans also work fewer hours a week than many of the most productive nations. The average work week is 40.2 hours in Japan, 40.1 hours in Germany, and 34.7 hours in the United States.[46]

Survey respondents' evaluations of the impact of alcohol and drug abuse in the workplace, and the extent to which employees strongly identify with the company, 1990 (in both cases, 0 = low, 100 = high):

COUNTRY	SUBSTANCE ABUSE	IDENTIFICATION
United States	**60.0**	**56.4**
Canada	50.6	52.2
Australia	47.6	46.9
Spain	44.4	45.0
Sweden	44.4	56.0
Switzerland	43.5	70.8
New Zealand	43.3	50.5
Denmark	43.2	68.4
Finland	42.7	60.4
Austria	42.3	68.6
Ireland	42.0	54.9
United Kingdom	41.5	48.2
France	40.6	57.9
Germany	40.4	64.3
Netherlands	39.0	58.5
Belgium[47]	38.1	61.1
Norway	36.3	60.7
Italy	31.2	46.7
Japan	24.8	84.7

Source: *World Competitiveness Report 1991*, published by IMD International, Lausanne, Switzerland, and World Economic Forum, Geneva, Switzerland, pp. 299, 347, 353.

SALARIES AND VACATIONS

- **We're Number One in executive salaries.**
- **We're Number One in inequality of pay.**

American chief executives make about twice as much as their counterparts abroad *and* twenty-five times more than the average American worker—the largest ratio of any of the nineteen major industrial nations. Average remuneration (salary, benefits, holdings, etc.) for a Japanese CEO is $371,800, less than half that of the average American CEO, $747,500. France's top executives are a distant second with an average remuneration of $448,500.

Salary differences are even more stark among chief executives at the top thirty companies in respective nations: Americans make $3.2 million on average, compared to $1.1 million in the United Kingdom, $800,000 in France and Germany, and $500,000 in Japan. While high executive salaries were once the pride of corporate America, the top-heavy pay structure is drawing criticism from many in the industry. "It's typical of what's wrong with American management," says one executive, "and why the U.S. is not more competitive economically."[48]

Average remuneration of chief executive officers (CEOs), and CEO remuneration as a multiple of average manufacturing employee remuneration, 1991:[49]

COUNTRY	CEO SALARIES (U.S. DOLLARS)	RATIO: CEO TO WORKER
United States	**$747,500**	**25**
France	448,500	16
Switzerland	424,100	11
Italy	421,300	14
Canada	407,600	12
United Kingdom	399,600	16
Belgium	397,300	13
Spain	380,600	15
Japan	371,800	11
Germany	364,500	10
Sweden	335,600	10
Netherlands	297,900	10
Australia	271,300	14
Ireland	156,500	8

Source: *Worldwide Total Remuneration 1991* (Valhalla, N.Y.: Towers Perrin, 1991), pp. 12, 22.

• **We're Last in paid vacation days.**

Vacations give us time for friends and family, as well as an
opportunity to recover from the mental anguish of a pressured
workplace. Even physical illness can be staved off by a little rest
and relaxation. Americans receive an average of about eleven
paid vacation days a year, the least of any citizens in the nineteen major industrial nations for which data is available. Spain
offers the most paid vacation days, an average of 32 per year.
Close to thirty days of vacation each year is the average in the
Netherlands, Norway, Finland, Sweden, France, and Germany,
as well.

Paid vacation days per year, 1991:

COUNTRY[50]	VACATION DAYS	COUNTRY	VACATION DAYS
Spain	32.0	Belgium	24.6
Netherlands	31.9	Italy	24.6
Norway	31.4	United Kingdom	24.5
Germany	29.9	Japan	24.0
Finland	28.6	Switzerland	23.4
Sweden	27.8	Ireland	22.9
France	27.0	Australia	22.4
Austria	26.8	Canada	14.7
Denmark	25.0	**United States**	**10.8**

Source: Union Bank of Switzerland, *Prices and Earnings Around the Globe, 1991* (Zurich: UBS, 1991),
p. 8.

DEMOCRACY'S BUREAUCRACIES

POLITICS

With the collapse of communism, American democracy has become the model for nations shedding their authoritarian skin. Ironically, while the world audience is captivated by our political system, U.S. citizens are largely uninterested. "Americans view politics with boredom and detachment," says E. J. Dionne in *Why Americans Hate Politics*. "For most of us, politics is increasingly abstract, a spectator sport barely worth watching."[1]

While American democracy may seem utopian from afar, up close it is riddled with contradictions and problems. For example, what do we make of a nation where the average senatorial candidate spends more than $3 million to get elected? Where political action committees (PACs) contribute $160 million to congressional campaigns "to obtain special access and influence," including more than $6 million to *unopposed* candidates?[2] As the disparity grows between the democracy we promote abroad and the democracy we experience at home, the American people are rightfully becoming suspicious. The savings and loan crisis, budget haggling, and ethics scandals are undermining the public's confidence in government. Only 23 percent of Americans say they approve of the way Congress has done its job, down from 42 percent in 1987.[3] Seven out of ten Americans say they think elected officials make too much money (47 percent say they make "a *lot* too much").[4]

Is politics inevitably the realm of corruption and inefficiency—or at least unfulfilled expectations? Some political commentators think so. "Giving money and power to government," says P. J. O'Rourke, "is like giving whiskey and car keys to teenage boys."[5]

VOTING

- **We're Number One in percentage of population who say they take an active interest in politics.**
- **We're Last in voter turnout.**

Americans lead in saying they take an active interest in politics and yet we are last in voter turnout among the nineteen major industrial nations. Eighty percent of Americans say they take some interest in politics, according to the World Values Survey, and 11.5 percent say they take an active interest, such as working for a candidate or registering voters. On average, 6 percent of respondents in the nineteen major industrial nations, about half as many as in America, say they take an active interest in politics.

Unfortunately, our few active participants can't compensate for the half of the American electorate that doesn't show up at the polls. In the 1988 presidential election, 50 percent of eligible Americans voted—a smaller share than in national elections in the remainder of the nineteen major industrial nations.[6] Voter turnout in the United States, according to census surveys, is highest among people age 65 and over (68.8 percent). Next, with 67.9 percent, are those age 45 to 64. Eighteen- to twenty-years-olds are last, with 33.2 percent voting.[7] The number of Americans who *say* they vote is about thirteen million more than actually do.[8]

Percentage of respondents who say they take an active interest in politics, 1981–83, and voter turnout in national elections as a percentage of eligible voters, 1971–88:[9]

COUNTRY	ACTIVE INTEREST	VOTER TURNOUT
United States	**11.5**	**50**
Finland	9.0	82
Canada	7.2	67
Sweden	7.1	87
France	6.5	77
Germany	6.4	84
United Kingdom[10]	5.6	75
Norway	5.0	81
Italy	4.9	93
Ireland	4.4	77
Spain	4.4	78
Denmark	4.2	87
Japan	3.7	73
Belgium	3.3	88
Netherlands	2.8	82

Sources: World Values Survey; Robert W. Jackman, "Political Institutions and Voter Turnout In the Industrial Democracies," *American Political Science Review*, vol. 81, no. 2, June 1987.

Universal suffrage—or suffering?

Voter turnout in America is lower than in other nations in part because it is harder for citizens to register to vote in the United States. As a result, only about 70 percent of eligible Americans are registered, compared to 85 percent or more of eligible citizens in the remainder of the nineteen major industrial nations. In these countries, the government facilitates the registration of voters, either by automatic registration or some other legal impetus. For example, in Australia and New Zealand, registering is required by law and nonregistrants are subject to fines. In France, while the burden is on the voters, citizens are required to get identification cards in their community, thus facilitating the registration process. Registering to vote in the United States can be truly byzantine. Residency requirements, and the fact that about half of all Americans move at least once every five years, make it difficult for many people to register. Recently, some politicians have been calling for reforms such as on-site registration on election day and automatic "motor voter" registration via driver's licenses.

Sources: G. Bingham Powell, "American Voter Turnout in Comparative Perspective," *American Political Science Review*, vol. 80, no. 1, March 1986; U.S. Bureau of the Census, *Statistical Abstract of the United States 1991* (Washington, D.C.: USGPO, 1991), p. 269.

DIVERSITY

- **We're Number One in ethnic diversity.**
- **We're Number 11 in tolerance of people with different ideas.**

Whether it's a melting pot or a mixed salad, the United States is the most ethnically diverse of the nineteen major industrial nations and one of the most diverse nations on earth. From the arrival of the Puritans at Plymouth Rock in the early seventeenth century, to the later mass immigrations of Italians, Irish, and Jews, to the more recent arrival of Dominicans, Salvadorans, Cubans, Haitians, Nigerians, Laotians, Cambodians, Vietnamese, and Koreans, a unique ethnic landscape has been built in the United States.

Unfortunately, diversity seems to have bred almost as much intolerance as pride among Americans. The United States ranks Number 11 in tolerance of people whose ideas, beliefs, or values are different from our own. While the majority of Americans polled (59 percent) have no qualms about spending time with different types of people, more than 40 percent say they have some reservations about (and almost a quarter of these say they dislike "quite a lot" or "very much") being with people with different ideas and values. Denmark, whose population is almost 100 percent Scandinavian in origin, is the most tolerant nation, according to the survey. But homogeneity doesn't automatically foster tolerance. Japan, with virtually no ethnic minorities, is among the least tolerant of all those nations surveyed.

Percentage of respondents answering "Not at all" to the question, "Do you dislike being with people whose ideas, beliefs, or values are different from your own?," 1981–83:

COUNTRY	FULLY TOLERANT OF OTHER PEOPLE	COUNTRY	FULLY TOLERANT OF OTHER PEOPLE
Denmark	85.4	Finland	62.0
France	73.8	Italy	61.2
United Kingdom''	71.8	Belgium	59.7
Netherlands	68.2	**United States**	**58.9**
Norway	67.7	Germany	57.0
Canada	63.7	Spain	42.3
Ireland	63.3	Japan	13.3

Source: World Values Survey.

GOVERNMENT EFFICIENCY

- **We're Number 17 in efficient government use of natural resources.**

The United States is often thought to have boundless natural resources upon which it can rely for agriculture, industry, and recreation. While many of our reserves are abundant because of the sheer size of our nation, the United States receives one of the lowest ratings in government efficiency in use of natural resources, according to a recent worldwide survey of business leaders. Only Spain and Italy receive lower marks. The Netherlands, Switzerland, and New Zealand top the list.

Average ratings (on an ascending scale of 1–100) of the effectiveness of government in managing the use and allocation of public natural resources, the nineteen major industrial nations, 1990:

COUNTRY	RESOURCE USE	COUNTRY	RESOURCE USE
Netherlands	59.6	Belgium[12]	52.9
Switzerland	59.4	Ireland	52.5
New Zealand	59.1	Australia	52.4
Sweden	58.8	Denmark	52.2
Finland	58.6	France	51.5
Canada	58.0	Austria	51.3
Norway	57.4	**United States**	**50.9**
Japan	55.6	Italy	44.1
Germany	55.0	Spain	43.3
United Kingdom	53.0		

Source: *World Competitiveness Report 1991*, published by IMD International, Lausanne, Switzerland, and World Economic Forum, Geneva, Switzerland, p. 289.

WOMEN

- **We're Number 15 in women's wages as a percentage of men's.**

Four out of five Americans say they would vote for a woman for president. Two thirds of Americans say they still support the Equal Rights Amendment despite Congress's failure to enact it.[13] Yet decades after the birth of the American women's movement and the struggle for equal opportunity and treatment, women of fourteen nations are better paid than their American counterparts relative to men's wages.

For every dollar an American man makes, a woman makes 74 cents on average (66 cents when part-time work is included). In Japan, for every dollar a man makes, a woman makes 50 cents. Australia, Denmark, France, New Zealand, Sweden, and Italy are the most equitable of the nineteen major industrial nations in terms of compensation; women in these nations—and in Kenya—make 80 cents or more on each male dollar. In Iceland, women make 91 cents per male dollar.

Women's average wage as a percentage of men's average wage, 1986–91:[14]

COUNTRY	WOMEN'S WAGES	COUNTRY	WOMEN'S WAGES
Iceland	91	Belgium	75
Australia	88	Norway	75
Denmark	83	**United States**	**74**
France	82	Germany	73
New Zealand	81	Czechoslovakia	70
Sweden	81	United Kingdom	70
Italy	80	Switzerland	67
Kenya	80	Greece	65
Austria	78	Luxembourg	63
Netherlands	77	Canada	63
Finland	76	Ireland	62
Portugal	76	Japan	50

Sources: International Labor Organization, *Yearbook of Labor Statistics 1989–90* (Geneva: ILO, 1990), pp. 757–65; United Nations Development Programme, *Human Development Report* (New York: Oxford University Press, 1991), p. 179; U.S. Bureau of Labor Statistics.

• We're Number 63 in women legislators.

A woman's place is in the house, it has been said, and in the senate. While this adage may have been born in America, it seems to apply more accurately abroad, particularly in the sixty-two countries that have a larger share of women legislators than we do. Among the nineteen major industrial nations, only Japan has a smaller percentage of women in its legislature than America.

While women make up more than half of America's population, they constitute less than 6 percent of the U.S. Congress and 12 percent of all executive office positions in the federal government. The absence of women legislators was glaringly evident during the confirmation hearings of Supreme Court Justice Clarence Thomas in October 1991, when Professor Anita Hill accused Thomas of sexual harassment. Hill and Thomas were questioned by members of the Senate Judiciary Committee, all of whom were men.

Women are better represented in almost all developed nations and in many developing nations as well, including Grenada, Panama, and Iraq. The most equitable ratios are found in the Soviet Union and its former satellites, and in the Scandinavian countries. In Pakistan, where Benazir Bhutto became the first female prime minister of an Islamic country, twenty seats in the parliament are reserved for women.

Countries with women occupying 20 percent or more of the parliamentary seats, 1987–91:

COUNTRY	WOMEN LAWMAKERS	COUNTRY	WOMEN LAWMAKERS
Soviet Union	34.5	Mongolia	24.9
Norway	34.4	Seychelles	24.0
Romania	34.4	China	21.2
Cuba	33.9	North Korea	21.1
East Germany	32.2	Bulgaria	21.0
Finland	31.5	Hungary	21.0
Czechoslovakia	29.5	Poland	20.2
Denmark	29.1	Netherlands	20.0
Albania	28.8		
Sweden	28.5	**United States**	**5.8**

Sources (for chart and text): *The World's Women 1970–1990: Trends and Statistics* (New York: United Nations, 1991), pp. 39–42. U.S.: League of Women Voters.

INTERNATIONAL

- **We're Number One in U.N. dues outstanding.**
- **We're Number One in U.N. Security Council vetoes since 1980.**

The United States continues to flip-flop on support for the United Nations. During the Persian Gulf war, President Bush praised the U.N.'s role in the American-led coalition against Iraq. At the same time, the United States owes more than a quarter of a billion dollars in dues to the U.N., more than five times the amount owed by the former Soviet Union, the next worst offender. In addition, the United States cast the most U.N. Security Council vetoes during the last decade, establishing itself—justifiably or not—as the most stalwart of the five permanent member nations. The two facts are probably not unrelated; until the 1980s, the Soviet Union led overwhelmingly in Security Council vetoes and was the most negligent in paying its annual dues.

President Bush says he's going to make good on President Reagan's 1988 pledge to pay back all outstanding U.N. dues. But the $300 million that the United States contributed to the U.N. in 1991 covered our debts only through 1990. U.S. dues for 1991 are still largely unpaid and our 1992 payment is already late. Of the nineteen major industrial nations, only the United States has dues outstanding from a previous year.[15]

Total outstanding United Nations dues, top ten offenders as of December 31, 1991, and the percentage of all U.N. assessments for which that country is responsible, 1992:

COUNTRY	DUES OUTSTANDING[16]	COUNTRY'S SHARE OF TOTAL (%)
United States	**$266,407,875**	**25.00**
USSR	46,019,313	9.41
South Africa	45,007,168	0.11
Brazil	17,823,960	1.59
Argentina	14,019,884	0.57
Yugoslavia	7,850,297	0.42
Iran	6,708,766	0.77
Ukraine	5,758,172	1.18
Israel	3,827,994	0.23
Turkey	2,896,285	0.27

Source: United Nations, Office of the Spokesman.

Security council vetoes, 1980–91:[17]

COUNTRY	VETOES SINCE 1980	VETOES SINCE 1946
United States	**48**	**69**
USSR	4	114
China	0	3
United Kingdom	15	32
France	7	18

Source: United States Mission to the United Nations.

- **We're Number One in membership in human rights groups.**
- **We're Number One in NOT ratifying international human rights treaties.**

One in twenty Americans is a member of an organization concerned with human rights at home or abroad, according to the World Values Survey. That gives the United States more human rights activists per capita than any other country for which data is available. Yet the United States has ratified fewer of the three major human rights treaties of the last quarter century than any of the nineteen major industrial nations. America has *signed* the International Covenant on Civil and Political Rights (ICCPR), the International Covenant on Economic, Social and Cultural Rights (ICESCR), and the United Nations Convention against Torture and Other Cruel, Inhuman or Degrading Treatment or Punishment.[18] But because we ratified only the U.N. Convention against Torture (in October 1990, three years after it went into effect), we are the only one of the nineteen major industrial nations that has not *ratified* at least two of these treaties.[19] Australia, Austria, Canada, Denmark, Finland, France, Germany, Italy, the Netherlands, New Zealand, Norway, Spain, Sweden, and the U.K. have signed and ratified all three accords. Even Iraq, however facetiously, ratified two of the three treaties.

According to Amnesty International, countries that ratify human rights treaties are bound to observe their provisions; signatories are obliged only to "refrain from acts which would defeat the object and purpose of the treaty."[20] In other words, signatories are not really bound to comply. Why has the United States signed but not ratified two of these three vital human rights accords? According to Amnesty officials, the ICCPR and ICESCR—both of which went into effect fifteen years ago—have not been ratified in the United States because of political opposition in Congress.[21]

Actions of various nations on the International Covenant on Civil and Political Rights (ICCPR), the International Covenant on Economic, Social and Cultural Rights (ICESCR), and the United Nations Convention against Torture and Other Cruel, Inhuman or Degrading Treatment or Punishment, 1991. Key: S = Signed, R = Ratified, X = No Action:

COUNTRY	ICCPR[22]	ICESCR	U.N./TORTURE
Australia	R	R	R
Austria	R	R	R
Canada	R	R	R
Denmark	R	R	R
Finland	R	R	R
France	R	R	R
Germany	R	R	R
Italy	R	R	R
Netherlands	R	R	R
New Zealand	R	R	R
Norway	R	R	R
Spain	R	R	R
Sweden	R	R	R
United Kingdom	R	R	R
Belgium	R	R	S
Ireland	R	R	X
Japan	R	R	X
United States	S	S	R

Source: *Amnesty International Report 1991* (New York: Amnesty International, 1991), pp. 240, 273–77.

• We're Number 13 in peace-keeping forces.

The United States contributes a smaller percentage of its military personnel to international peace-keeping forces than all but one of the nineteen major industrial nations for which data is available. Less than one tenth of one percent (0.06 percent) of our forces are involved in United Nations peace work. Ireland, the leading contributor, lends nearly 7 percent of its military personnel to peace-keeping activities.

Peace-keeping forces as a percentage of all military personnel, 1989:

COUNTRY	PEACE-KEEPING	COUNTRY	PEACE-KEEPING
Ireland	6.7	New Zealand	0.4
Finland	6.1	United Kingdom	0.3
Norway	2.6	France	0.1
Austria	2.3	Netherlands	0.1
Canada	1.4	Italy	0.06
Denmark	1.4	**United States**	**0.06**
Sweden	1.2	Spain	0.03
Australia	0.5		

Source: Michael Kidron and Dan Smith, *The New State of War and Peace* (New York: Touchstone, 1991), pp. 20–21.

TRIALS AND TRIBULATIONS

CRIME AND THE LEGAL SYSTEM

Violent crime has become a fixed element of American life, particularly for city dwellers. Murder, rape, assault, and theft are on the rise; more than half of Americans surveyed say they have been the victim of a crime in the last five years.

Our high crime rate produces an array of serious problems. Victims, and those close to them, suffer physical and emotional pain, loss, and trauma. Our correctional system is burdened by lengthy trials and overcrowded prisons. Growing expenditures on police and new prisons cut deeper into the government's already strained domestic budget, even as 70 percent of Americans say that the government is spending too little on crime control.[1] Private security measures, including guards, alarms, and video surveillance, cost billions of dollars more annually.

Crime is making Americans thick-skinned and retributive. When asked what is the most important thing that can be done to reduce crime, Americans answer: harsher punishment.[2] More than a quarter of our homes are armed with handguns (double the rate of the next highest country), we've lost the ability to rehabilitate most prisoners, and we've reinstituted the death penalty while other democracies have effectively abandoned it. Finally, the United States has experienced a huge increase in litigation, which some Americans find nearly as threatening to the future of our nation as our spiraling crime rate.

VICTIMIZATION

- **We're Number One in percentage of population who have been the victim of a crime.**

America leads the nineteen major industrial nations in percentage of people who say they have been the victim of a crime. Almost 30 percent of U.S. survey respondents say they have experienced a crime in the last year, and more than half say they have been victimized during the last five years. The American paradox continues; in the words of one recent study, "the wealthiest society in the world has failed to provide a relatively safe society; instead it has an appallingly high level of crime."[3]

Each nation has its own criminal bêtes noires. Canada leads in percentage of inhabitants who've experienced car vandalism and personal theft; Australia leads in percentage of people who've been the victim of burglary with entry and assault with force; the Netherlands in bicycle thefts; and the United States in homicide, sexual assault, attempted burglary, theft from car, and assault.

Percentage of population who say they have been the victim of a crime in the last year, 1989:

COUNTRY	PERCENT VICTIMIZED	COUNTRY	PERCENT VICTIMIZED
United States	**28.8**	United Kingdom[4]	19.4
Canada	28.1	Belgium	17.7
Australia	27.8	Norway	16.5
Netherlands	26.8	Finland	15.9
Spain	24.6	Switzerland	15.6
Germany	21.9	Japan[5]	9.3
France	19.4		

Source: Jan J. M. van Dijk et al., *Experiences of Crime across the World,* 2nd ed. (Deventer, the Netherlands: Kluwer, 1991), p. 174.

Silent victims.

About half of all victims do not report the crimes committed against them to police or other authorities. Rates of reporting are lowest for sex-related crimes and highest for car thefts.

Percentage of the following crimes reported to the police internationally, 1988:

CRIME	PERCENT REPORTED	CRIME	PERCENT REPORTED
Theft of car	93.2	Personal theft	40.7
Theft of motorcycle	85.4	Car vandalism	38.6
Burglary with entry	76.9	Assault/threat	30.7
Theft from car	62.2	Sexual incidents	9.9
Theft of bicycle	60.5		
Robbery	49.0	All crimes	49.6

Source: Jan J. M. van Dijk et al., *Experiences of Crime across the World*, 2nd ed. (Deventer, the Netherlands: Kluwer, 1991), p. 177.

MURDER AND DEATH

- **We're Number One in ranking the importance of God in our lives.**
- **We're Number One in murder.**

How can a God-fearing nation like the United States lead in murders per capita? When asked to rank the importance of God in their lives on an ascending scale of one to ten, 52 percent of Americans give God a ten, compared to 42 percent of Irish respondents, 34 percent of Canadians, and 17 percent of the Spanish. Overall, we turn up the most pious average (8.21) of the nineteen major industrial nations.[6] America is also Number One in percentage of population who believe that the commandment "Thou shalt not kill" still applies.[7]

Despite our piety, we commit more than twenty thousand murders a year, or about one murder every twenty-five minutes.

Rates are rising in big and small cities alike; Milwaukee and New Orleans experienced more than a 100 percent increase in murders between 1985 and 1990.[8] Many of these homicides are drug related, and an alarming number involve young Americans, particularly young black males. Our murder rate is more than twice as high as Germany's and nearly eight times as high as Japan's. Not only does that make us Number One in murders per capita, it may give us the unique distinction of being the most devout and sinful nation on earth, all at once.

Total number of murder cases, and murder cases per 100,000 population reported to police, 1988–90:

COUNTRY	MURDERS	PER 100,000
United States	**23,438**	**9.4**
Sweden	611	7.2
Canada	1,411	5.5
Denmark	265	5.2
France	2,567	4.6
Australia	738	4.5
Germany	2,543	4.2
Belgium	277	2.8
Spain	887	2.3
Switzerland	149	2.3
Italy	1,255	2.2
Norway	84	2.0
United Kingdom	992	2.0
Austria	139	1.8
Japan	1,441	1.2
Ireland	34	1.0
Finland	33	0.7

Source: Interpol.[9]

• We're Number One in the murder of children.

"Youth comes but once in a lifetime," wrote Henry Wadsworth Longfellow.[10] But for thousands of American children each year, youth comes not even once, and it is taken violently. Despite our children's deteriorating health, the disparity in mortality rates between youth in America and other nations is largely due to *unnatural* causes like accidents, suicide, and homicide. Three quarters of all young adult deaths are violent deaths.[11] In fact, the United States leads the nineteen major industrial nations in homicide among children age 1 to 19, and among males age 15 to 24. Willful neglect, child abuse, and stray inner-city bullets take young lives. In the category of young men age 15 to 24, which accounts for about a fifth of all American homicides, three quarters of murders are caused by firearms and many are drug related.

Black children age 1 to 19 are three times as likely as other American youth to be the victim of murder. The homicide rate among black young men age 15 to 24 (85.6 per 100,000) is seven times as high as the rate for white men the same age (11.2 per 100,000), which nonetheless is more than double the rate in New Zealand, the country with the next highest rate. Indeed, more black youth age 15 to 24 die as a result of homicide than from any other cause; motor vehicle accidents are the major cause of death for American youth in general.

Mortality rate per 100,000 due to homicide for children age 1 to 19, 1983–86, and for males age 15 to 24, 1986–87:

COUNTRY[12]	CHILDREN AGE 1–19	MALES AGE 15–24
U.S. black	**10.7**	**85.6**
United States	**3.7**	**21.9**
Denmark	1.5	1.0
Canada	1.1	2.9
Switzerland	1.0	1.4
Belgium	0.9	1.7
Germany	0.8	1.0
Norway	0.7	3.3
France	0.5	1.4
United Kingdom	0.5	1.2
Netherlands	0.4	1.4
Spain	0.3	—
Ireland	0.2	1.3
New Zealand	—	4.4
Finland	—	3.0
Australia	—	2.5
Sweden	—	2.3
Japan	—	0.5

Sources (for chart and text): Bret C. Williams and C. Arden Miller, *Preventive Health Care for Young Children* (Arlington, Va.: National Center for Clinical Infant Programs, 1991), p. 73; Lois A. Fingerhut and Joel C. Kleinman, "International and Interstate Comparisons of Homicide Among Young Males," *JAMA*, vol. 263, no. 24, June 27, 1990. p. 3293.

- **We're Number 14 in percentage of murders solved.**
- **We're Number One in murderers still at large.**

Are American policemen spending too much time tracking down coffee and doughnuts instead of criminals? While the sleuths at Scotland Yard are edged out by the Japanese in percentage of murder cases solved, America's detectives aren't even in the running. Thirty percent of the murder cases reported in the United States in 1988 have not been solved, according to Interpol. That makes us Number 14 in percentage of murders solved; only two of the nineteen major industrial nations do worse. And in absolute terms, it means we have the most murderers at large. Perhaps that's one reason television programs like

America's Most Wanted and *Unsolved Mysteries* have become so popular; with about five thousand murderers from 1988 alone still at large, it's in our own best interest to join in the search.

Percentage of murder cases solved by the police, 1988:

COUNTRY	MURDERS SOLVED	COUNTRY	MURDERS SOLVED
Japan	97.1	Canada	86.0
United Kingdom	95.0	Spain	86.0
Germany	94.4	France	83.1
Finland	93.9	Norway	83.0
Austria	93.5	Belgium	77.2
Australia	91.6	**United States**	**70.0**
Ireland	91.2	Sweden	59.0
Denmark	89.4	Italy	39.0

Source: Interpol.

- **We're Number One in deaths by gun.**
- **We're Number One in deaths by capital punishment.**

With an estimated two hundred million guns at our disposal, there are enough weapons to arm every adult in the United States. It's no wonder, then, that guns account for a greater proportion of murders in the United States than in any other nation for which data is available. Firearms account for 60 percent of all murders.[13]

As fatal shootings increase throughout the nation, gun control has become a major issue. Eight out of ten Americans say laws covering the sale of firearms should be more strict, and 95 percent support the measure passed by Congress in 1991 requiring a seven-day waiting period on handgun purchases.[14] The public's increasing support for gun control is probably related to the sad fact that the United States leads other nations in handgun deaths by such a huge margin (our rate is almost one hundred times that of Japan). Even when restricted to homicide, the per capita handgun death rate in the United States is almost five times that of the next highest country, Switzerland. Gun control laws in other nations are much stricter than in the United States. In Japan and the United Kingdom, handguns are essentially prohibited, except for gun collectors and members of licensed clubs. In Australia, Canada, and Switzerland, thorough background checks are required, and in Germany and Sweden handgun licenses are extremely difficult to obtain.

Handgun death is, to some degree, a form of violence that we will never be able to fully control. Even if guns were completely prohibited, determined criminals would find a way to get them. Deaths that occur as a result of capital punishment are a different story. Electrocution, lethal injection, gas chamber, or firing squad: take your pick. The United States is Number One in capital punishment because we are the only Western industrial nation that still uses the death penalty on a regular basis.[15] The U.S. Supreme Court reinstated the death penalty in 1976, overturning a 1972 decision that had outlawed the death penalty on the grounds that it was unconstitutional. Since the reinstatement of capital punishment, more than 150 men have been executed, mostly in eleven southern states. Twenty-three were put to death in 1990.[16] More than two thousand are now on death row.[17]

The death penalty is currently used by thirty-six states and by the federal government in cases of first-degree murder with aggravated circumstances, such as the death of a law enforcement officer. A 1988 federal provision expanded circumstances under which the death penalty can be applied to include murder in the course of a major drug operation. In April 1991, the first death sentence was imposed under this new federal statute.

Three quarters of Americans surveyed favor the death penalty for persons convicted of murder.[18] One in three say they "would actually volunteer to pull the switch for an electric-chair execution," according to a recent study of American values.[19] Advocates support the death penalty not only as a form of punishment but as a deterrent to other criminals. Some supporters of the death penalty also point out the high cost of life imprisonment (as much as $30,000 per year in some states) that can be averted by capital punishment. Opponents argue that the death penalty has not deterred crime and that the cost of litigating death penalty appeals is greater than the cost of imprisoning a convict for life.

While the Supreme Court suggested in 1976 that the death penalty could be applied without bias or arbitrariness, many opponents argue that the U.S. system of capital punishment is still racist. "Though blacks are homicide victims at a rate six times greater than whites, 95 percent of those executed in 1990 murdered white people," according to the Death Penalty Information Center.[20] In fact, while more than forty blacks who killed whites have been executed in the last fifteen years, no white who killed a black person received the same fate until September 1991.

Number of people killed with handguns, 1988–90:

COUNTRY	TOTAL	PER MILLION
United States	**9,602**	**38.3**
Switzerland	53	7.9
Israel	25	5.7
Sweden	19	2.3
Australia	13	0.8
Japan[21]	46	0.4
Canada	8	0.3
United Kingdom	7	0.1

Sources: Handgun Control, Inc. (Washington, D.C.); U.S. Department of Justice, *Uniform Crime Reports 1990* (Washington, D.C.: USGPO, 1991), p. 12; Text: Handgun Control, Inc. and the Death Penalty Information Center (Washington, D.C.).

RAPE

- **We're Number One in reported rapes.**

Rape awareness has increased in the United States in recent years, in part because of efforts to encourage rape victims to come forward and hold sexual assaulters accountable for their actions. The much-publicized trial of William Kennedy Smith brought increased attention to acquaintance rape, in particular.

As many as eight out of ten women who are raped know their attacker.[22] More than one quarter of all rapes occur in or near the home of the person being assaulted, and another 15 percent occur at the home of a friend, relative, or neighbor.[23] While the reported annual rate of rape in the United States is 114 per 100,000 population, the highest rate of any nation for which data is available, a recent study finds that 21 percent of American women say they have been raped since age 14.[24] Converted to an annual rate, this figure would be more than ten times as high as the reported rate. In another study, more than one in eight white young American women (12.7 percent) say they were raped by age 20. One in seventeen say they were raped at age 14 or younger.[25]

Some observers might conclude that America has the highest prevalence of rape only because the crime is reported more regularly in the United States than elsewhere. The data, however, does not support this assumption. While rape is the most underreported crime throughout the world, the reporting rate in America for sexual assault—about one in eight cases—is only a little above average.[26] Rape is more fully reported in Belgium, the Netherlands, and Scotland. Therefore, the large gap between the number of reported rapes in the United States and other nations is probably an accurate reflection of the proliferation of this violent crime in our country.

Reported rapes per 100,000 women age 15 to 59, 1980–85:

COUNTRY	RATE	COUNTRY	RATE
United States	**114**	Poland	14
Netherlands	92	France	11
Finland	40	Italy	10
Sweden	34	Norway	10
Canada	30	United Kingdom	9
Yugoslavia	27	Spain	8
Israel	25	Japan	7
New Zealand	24	Ireland	4
Denmark	20	Portugal	4

Source: United Nations Development Programme, *Human Development Report 1991* (New York: Oxford University Press, 1991), p. 176.

DRUGS AND DRUNK DRIVING

- **We're Number One in drug offenders per capita.**
- **We're Number One in marijuana and cocaine seized per capita.**

In recent years, drug use has become a primary concern of the American public.[27] Americans are ten times more likely to cite drugs as the major factor responsible for crime than the next most frequent response, breakdown of family and social values.[28] More than a million drug arrests are made each year, giving the United States the highest rate of drug offenders of any of the nineteen major industrial nations. Sweden, Switzerland, and Denmark have the most drug offenders after the United States, while Japan and Ireland have about three hundred times *fewer* drug criminals. Drug offenders account for more than half (58 percent) of all persons incarcerated in federal institutions in the United States; more than half of all state prison inmates were under the influence of drugs or alcohol when they committed their crime.[29] The social and economic costs of drug abuse have increased markedly—to an estimated $60 billion a year.[30]

In addition to leading in drug offenders, the United States is

Number One in marijuana and cocaine seized among the nineteen major industrial nations. Only major drug-producing nations like Colombia and small drug-trafficking ports such as the Bahamas seize more drugs per capita.[31] The United States confiscates about four times as much marijuana and cocaine per capita as the major industrial nations with the next highest rates respectively. In relative terms, we seize more than ten times as much marijuana as the United Kingdom and France, more than a hundred times as much as Germany, and more than two thousand times as much as Japan. America also seizes twenty times as much cocaine per person as the U.K. and Germany (Japan doesn't even make it onto the map here).

Number of drug offenders per 100,000 population, 1988:[32]

COUNTRY	DRUG OFFENDERS	COUNTRY	DRUG OFFENDERS
United States	**346**	Spain	72
Sweden	311	Belgium	63
Switzerland	283	Austria	58
Denmark	253	United Kingdom	56
Canada	167	Finland	42
Germany	110	Norway	30
France	87	Ireland	1
Italy	77	Japan	1

Source: Interpol.

Kilograms of marijuana and cocaine seized per 1 million people, 1983:[33]

COUNTRY	MARIJUANA KILOS/1,000,000	COCAINE KILOS/1,000,000[34]
United States	**3,485.7**	**38.1**
Canada	937.8	3.9
Netherlands	263.2	4.1
United Kingdom	247.0	1.7
France	229.1	4.2
Sweden	142.6	0.1
Australia	107.7	0.6
New Zealand	98.7	0.1
Belgium	86.2	2.5
Austria	66.1	0.2
Spain	53.2	7.2
Switzerland	25.3	8.1
Germany	20.5	1.7
Italy	18.0	3.9
Ireland	12.7	0.0
Denmark	5.2	7.1
Norway	2.6	0.0
Japan	1.6	0.0
Finland	1.5	—
USSR	0.1	—

Source: M. Adrian, P. Jull, R. Williams (comp.), *Statistics on Alcohol and Drug Use in Canada and Other Countries*, vol. 1: *Statistics on Alcohol Use* and vol. 2: *Statistics on Drug Use* (Toronto: Alcoholism and Drug Addiction Research Foundation, 1989), Table 1.41. Original: United Nations.

- **We're Number One in leniency toward drinking and driving.**
- **We're Number One in drunk-driving fatalities.**

Nearly one American in ten thousand dies each year as a result of drunk driving accidents, twice as many people as in Poland, the country with the next highest rate. The fact that we are Number One in drunk-driving fatalities per capita may not be surprising, considering that we're Number One in car travel and Number 4 in alcohol consumption. What is surprising is that we are the most lenient toward drunk driving of the nineteen major industrial nations.

While campaigns to stop drunk driving have proliferated in the United States in recent years, "our penalties continue to be minimal in comparison to other countries around the world," according to Mothers Against Drunk Driving (MADD). For example, a first-time drunk-driving offender in the United States can generally be imprisoned for zero to three days in addition to a fine and suspension of a driver's license. A first-time offender in France can be imprisoned anywhere from two months to two years. Furthermore, the crime is more narrowly defined in America than in other nations. In most of the United States it is illegal to drive with a blood alcohol content of .10 percent or more.[35] European countries generally define drunk driving more strictly at .05 to .08 percent of blood alcohol. In Japan, *any* trace of alcohol in the blood signifies impairment and can bring extreme punishments.

Number of people killed in car accidents due to drunk driving, and rate per 100,000 people, 1983–90:[36]

COUNTRY	NUMBER KILLED	PER 100,000
United States	**22,083**	**8.8**
Poland	1,614	4.4
West Germany	2,547	4.1
Denmark	191	3.7
Hungary	387	3.6
Austria	263	3.5
Switzerland	215	3.3
Finland	112	2.3
Yugoslavia	467	2.1
East Germany	309	1.9
Czechoslovakia	272	1.8
Netherlands	260	1.8
Sweden	95	1.1
Belgium	77	0.8
United Kingdom	379	0.7
Spain	174	0.5
Turkey	120	0.3

Sources: M. Adrian, P. Jull, R. Williams (comp.), *Statistics on Alcohol and Drug Use in Canada and Other Countries*, vol. 1: *Statistics on Alcohol Use* and vol. 2: *Statistics on Drug Use* (Toronto: Alcoholism and Drug Addiction Research Foundation, 1989), Table 1.29. Original: United Nations; Mothers Against Drunk Driving (MADD) (Dallas, Texas).

THEFT

- **We're Number One in percentage of population that believes that the commandment "Thou shalt not steal" still applies today.**
- **We're Number One in robbers and thieves per capita.**

Just as Americans lead the nineteen major industrial nations in believing in the commandment "Thou shalt not kill," we are also Number One in believing in the admonition "Thou shalt not steal." Again, this belief does not seem to correlate with our behavior. The United States is home to more robbers and thieves per capita than any of the nineteen major industrial nations. Spain is a close second, while the fewest robbers per capita are found in Japan, where citizens reportedly leave briefcases and shopping bags unguarded while they go about their daily business.[37]

Percentage of population that believes that the commandment "Thou shalt not steal" still applies fully, 1981–83, and number of persons per 100,000 who have committed robbery and/or violent theft, 1988:

COUNTRY	APPLIES FULLY	ROBBERS AND THIEVES PER 100,000
United States	**92.9**	**45**
Norway	92.7	3
Italy	92.6	13
Sweden	90.8	11
Canada	87.6	30
United Kingdom[38]	86.8	9
Japan	85.9	1
Germany	81.1	27
Spain	80.7	42
Finland	77.8	37
France	69.5	26

Sources: World Values Survey; Interpol.

GUNS

- **We're Number One in gun ownership.**
- **We're Number One in percentage of people who believe killing in self-defense can always be justified.**

More than one American household in four owns a handgun, the highest rate of any nation for which data is available. Handguns are four times as common in America as in Germany and more than seventy times as prevalent here as in the United Kingdom. In addition, America leads the nineteen major industrial nations in percentage of citizens who say that killing in self-defense can always be justified.

Almost half of all Americans (47 percent) have some kind of gun (rifle, handgun, etc.) in their home. More than four in ten American gun owners say their gun is loaded now, and nearly eight in ten have fired their gun at some time. A quarter of American gun owners say they carry the weapon on their person. Perhaps most interesting is the fact that twice as many gun owners say they have been threatened with a handgun (16 percent) as have used one in defense (8 percent).[39] Which is not to say that they *wouldn't* use their guns: 84 percent of Americans say it is at least sometimes justifiable to kill in self-defense, and 35 percent say it always is. The Japanese lead in saying that killing in self-defense can never be justified (62 percent).

Percentage of households with handguns, according to survey respondents, 1989, and percentage of people who say killing in self-defense can be justified sometimes or always, 1981–83:

COUNTRY	HAVE HANDGUNS	SELF-DEFENSE KILLING JUSTIFIABLE
United States	28.6	84.1
Switzerland	13.9	—
Finland	7.1	63.2
Germany	6.7	63.0
Belgium	6.4	69.0
France	5.9	82.5
Canada	5.2	82.8
Norway	3.7	73.0
Spain	2.2	80.4
Australia	1.6	86.8
Netherlands	0.9	75.7
United Kingdom[40]	0.4	73.1
Japan	—	38.3

Sources: Jan J. M. van Dijk et al., *Experiences of Crime across the World*, 2nd ed. (Deventer, the Netherlands: Kluwer, 1991); personal correspondence with Jan van Dijk; World Values Survey.

LAWYERS AND LITIGATION

- **We're Number One in lawyers.**
- **We're Number One in litigation.**

From the admonition in Shakespeare's *King Henry VI, Part II*, "Let's kill all the lawyers," to H. L. Mencken's claim that "a peasant between two lawyers is like a fish between two cats," the legal profession has often taken it on the chin.[41] Lately, the criticism has focused on law and international competition, as skeptics wonder if our slipping position in industry, finance, and health care might be linked to the fact that we are Number One in lawyers and litigation. In the summer of 1991, Vice-President Dan Quayle told a national convention of lawyers that America's current penchant for litigation was "a self-inflicted competitive disadvantage."[42]

The United States is home to almost eight hundred thousand lawyers, more than half of the world's total, according to the American Bar Association. At more than 300 lawyers per 100,000 population, America has more than twice as many lawyers per capita as Britain and almost four times as many as Germany. In formal terms, Japan has only 13 lawyers per 100,000 inhabitants, though their legal system includes many paralegals and specialists who carry out tasks performed by lawyers in America and elsewhere. Even when these other legal workers are included, Japan still has only a third the number of legal professionals per person as the United States. "People say we can't support them all," says law professor Marc Galanter, "but curiously we do."[43]

With our glut of lawyers, of course, comes a glut of litigation—the most of any nation in the world. Each year, eighteen million new civil lawsuits are initiated, at a total cost of as much as $300 billion a year, according to one government report.[44] That's more than the federal government spends on education annually. The number of federal lawsuits has almost tripled during the last thirty years; they regularly take as long as three to five years to resolve.

"[Litigation] is the special American burden, the one feature hardly anyone admires of a society that is otherwise envied the world around," Walter K. Olson writes in *The Litigation Explosion*.[45] Columnist Russell Baker cuts right to the chase: "This passion for converting all problems in human relations into lawsuits is another illustration of decay in the American character."[46] While litigation figures are not easily available from other nations, one study (see chart below) finds that the United States spends five times as much on personal injury litigation as its competitor nations, and that the cost of litigation grew between 1970 and 1986 the most in the United States. Excessive litigation leads to higher costs for businesses, higher prices for consumers, and worker layoffs from companies suffering liabilities.

Still, not all legal commentators feel that it is a bane for America to lead in litigation. One law professor writes: "Disputes are inevitable in a dynamic society with changing mores and a vibrant economy. . . . Here in America, unlike . . . Japan where there are severely lower ratios of lawyers to populace, most people are willing to take on the employer, the landlord, the big shot, or even the government itself—and the legal system enables them to do so.''[47]

Number of lawyers and lawyers per 100,000 people, 1986–91; and personal injury litigation costs as a percentage of GDP, 1986:[48]

COUNTRY	LAWYERS	PER 100,000	COST OF LITIGATION AS % OF GDP
United States	**777,119**	**310**	**2.6**
Finland	11,600	232	—
United Kingdom	83,987	147	0.5
Spain	51,254	131	0.4
USSR	300,000	104	—
Japan	16,341	93[49]	0.4
Norway	3,851	92	—
Belgium	8,500	87	0.6
Germany	62,000	80	0.5
Italy	40,000	70	0.5
Denmark	3,652	72	0.4
Netherlands	6,381	43	—
Ireland	1,500	41	—
Austria	2,887	38	0.6
France	18,000	32	0.6
Sweden	2,647	32	—

Sources: American Bar Association; Institute for Lawyers in Europe and *Lawyers in Europe,* Professional and Business Information, London (European nations); President's Council on Competitiveness, "Agenda for Civil Justice Reform in America." Litigation: *Tort Cost Trends: An International Perspective* (Simsbury, Ct.: Tillinghast, 1989), p. A11.

16,000 Lawyers Chase Ambulances On Air.

Some observers of the American legal profession ascribe the rising rate of litigation (particularly tort claims) in part to the growth of advertising by lawyers. Ambulance chasing, as lawyers' active solicitation of business is informally known, was once considered a transgression of legal ethics. In 1953, a major legal ethicist called the practice "so well known and so obviously improper as to require no extensive comment."[50] By the 1970s, solicitation had become commonplace, and in 1977 advertising by lawyers became legal. During the 1980s, lawyer advertising on television became widespread, spending increased 40 percent annually until it reached $82 million in 1989. Among the third of all lawyers in America who now advertise, 6 percent do so on television.

Among lawyers who advertise, percentage using various media, 1990:

MEDIUM	PERCENTAGE	MEDIUM	PERCENTAGE
Yellow pages	90	Radio	8
Newspapers	20	Direct mail	7
Magazines or journals	10	Television	6

Sources: David Gellman, "Developing Your Firm's Advertising and Marketing Strategy," *Lawyers Alert*, May 14, 1990, p. 19; Walter K. Olson, *The Litigation Explosion* (New York: Truman Talley, 1991), pp. 16–24.

BEHIND BARS

• We're Number One in incarceration.

There are more people behind bars in the United States than there are people living in San Francisco or Washington, D.C. With over one million inmates, the United States has a larger prison population and a higher rate of incarceration than any nation for which figures are recorded, according to The Sentencing Project, a nonprofit organization that promotes sentencing reform. Two notorious penal states, South Africa and the Soviet Union, fall far short of the U.S. rate of 426 inmates per

100,000 persons (that's one prisoner for every 235 Americans). Black males in the United States are imprisoned at a rate four times greater than black males in South Africa: 3,109 per 100,000 in the former, compared to 729 per 100,000 in the latter. In fact, nearly one in four black American men age 20 to 29 is currently incarcerated, on probation, or on parole.

Crackdowns on drug crimes, mandatory sentencing laws, and a high rate of recidivism have more than doubled our prison population since 1980, despite the fact that the crime rate *fell* slightly during the 1980s. The results: an annual cost of incarceration estimated at $16 billion and serious prison overcrowding. As many as forty states are now under federal court order to ease their overpopulated prisons, often through furlough and early-release programs that are unpopular with the public.

Rates of incarceration per 100,000 population, 1988–90:

COUNTRY	RATE	COUNTRY	RATE
United States	**426**	Austria	77
South Africa	333	Spain	76
Soviet Union	268	Finland	73
Hungary	196	Switzerland	73
Malaysia	126	Australia	72
Northern Ireland	120	Denmark	68
Hong Kong	118	Belgium	65
Poland	106	Italy	60
New Zealand	100	Sweden	56
United Kingdom	97	Ireland	55
Turkey	96	Norway	48
Germany	85	Japan	45
France	81	Netherlands	40

Sources (for chart and text): The Sentencing Project; Marc Mauer, "Americans Behind Bars: A Comparison of International Rates of Incarceration" (Washington, D.C.: The Sentencing Project, 1991); Council of Europe, *Prison Information Bulletin*, no. 15, June 1990, p. 6.

- **We're Number One in saying the aim of incarceration should be to protect citizens from prisoners.**
- **We're Last in saying the aim of incarceration should be to reeducate prisoners.**

Most of the major industrial nations seem to agree with the premise that the aim of imprisonment in a democratic society is to rehabilitate a prisoner, not just punish him. The majority of Americans, however, believe the primary purposes of incarceration are to protect citizens and "make those who have done wrong pay for it."[51] Given that America leads the major industrial nations in crime, including murder and rape, it may not be surprising that we're the toughest on criminals. Eight out of ten Americans think that courts are "not harsh enough." Eight out of ten also say that they're more worried that "some criminals are being let off too easily" than about the "abuse of constitutional rights" of the accused.[52]

Percentage of population who think the primary aim of imprisonment should be to protect citizens from prisoners, and percentage who think the aim should be to reeducate prisoners, 1981–83:

COUNTRY	PROTECT CITIZENS	REEDUCATE PRISONERS
United States	**32.4**	**27.4**
Canada	28.8	39.8
Australia	28.3	35.1
United Kingdom[53]	28.2	27.7
Ireland	24.7	41.5
Belgium	22.0	42.5
Finland	19.6	48.0
Netherlands	19.1	52.1
Germany	18.2	49.7
France	17.2	42.9
Denmark	16.0	35.7
Spain	12.4	57.5
Sweden	11.3	62.7
Norway	8.7	67.1
Japan	8.2	32.8
Italy	7.3	42.7

Source: World Values Survey.

GLUTTONS GALORE

THE ENVIRONMENT, ENERGY, AND TRANSPORTATION

We are a nation of nature-loving conservationists, or so we claim. Ninety-seven percent of Americans surveyed say the United States should be doing more to protect the environment and curb pollution; 87 percent of Americans support stronger action by international organizations such as the United Nations to stop pollution and prevent the loss of land, clean air, and water; and 84 percent say they are careful about protecting the environment and nature from destruction.[1] Eight out of ten even call themselves environmentalists.[2]

With this effusive national concern, one might assume that the United States fares well in international environmental comparisons. But again, what we say is not what we do. From global warming to acid rain, garbage disposal to oil dependency, we need to clean up our environmental act.

THE GREENHOUSE EFFECT

- **We're Number One in greenhouse gas emissions.**

Mother Earth will not tolerate her children's reckless ways much longer. Unregulated burning of fossil fuels, cement manufacturing, and deforestation have increased emissions of gases that promote the greenhouse effect, an environmental dilemma that could threaten life on earth as we know it. Are we getting the message? Perhaps, but the United States is still the Number One greenhouse culprit in the world.

The greenhouse effect is caused by the release into the atmosphere of carbon dioxide, methane, and chlorofluorocarbons (CFCs), as well as other gases such as tropospheric ozone and nitrous oxides. As these emissions continue to increase, more heat is trapped in the atmosphere, causing the earth's average temperature to rise. The repercussions of global warming for public health, animal life, agriculture, and water resources are potentially disastrous. The melting of polar ice caps could cause the sea level to rise substantially; some scientists even warn that major coastal cities could be flooded. "These emissions," according to *World Resources*, "could change our planet's climate, destroy the protective stratospheric ozone layer, acidify rainfall, and directly affect the health of people, plants and animals."[3]

Attempts to regulate emissions of greenhouse gases are under way. Reducing deforestation, particularly in Brazil and other countries in tropical rain forest regions, has become a priority for burgeoning environmental movements throughout the world. The United States and other nations have regulated the use of chlorofluorocarbons in aerosol cans, foam, refrigeration, and other products in an attempt to cut their use by half by the year 2000. Environmental advocates are encouraging the use of solar energy and hydrogen-based natural gases as alternatives to carbon-based fossil fuels such as coal and oil. But progress is slow; more cooperation and control are required to stave off these environmental dangers. "No one country or even one region can prevent the buildup of greenhouse gases by itself," *World Resources* says, "although leadership by individual countries will be important in achieving global consensus."[4] Indeed, the top five greenhouse contributors—the United States, the former Soviet Union, Brazil, China, and India—are responsible for 50 percent of the greenhouse gas emissions. In light of our contribution to the problem, we should lead the way toward a solution.

The Greenhouse Index: Twenty countries with the highest net emissions of greenhouse gases (carbon dioxide, methane, and chlorofluorocarbons) in thousand metric tons of carbon equivalent and percentage of world total, 1987:

COUNTRY	EMISSIONS	PERCENTAGE OF TOTAL
United States	**1,000,000**	**17.6**
Soviet Union	690,000	12.0
Brazil	610,000	10.5
China	380,000	6.6
India	230,000	3.9
Japan	220,000	3.9
West Germany	160,000	2.8
United Kingdom	150,000	2.7
Indonesia	140,000	2.4
France	120,000	2.1
Italy	120,000	2.1
Canada	120,000	2.0
Mexico	78,000	1.4
Myanmar	77,000	1.3
Poland	76,000	1.3
Spain	73,000	1.3
Colombia	69,000	1.2
Thailand	67,000	1.2
Australia	63,000	1.1
East Germany	62,000	1.1

Source (for chart and text): World Resources Institute, *World Resources 1990–91* (New York: Oxford University Press, 1990), p. 15.

AIR AND ATMOSPHERE

- **We're Number One in emissions of air pollutants per capita.**
- **We're Number One in contributing to acid rain.**

The average American is responsible for nearly six tons of carbon dioxide emissions annually from normal energy use.[5] That's the largest carbon dioxide emission per capita of any of the nineteen major industrial nations. Fossil fuel production and consumption accounts for the majority of human carbon dioxide emissions, which, in turn, have the largest impact of any gas on the greenhouse effect.

The United States also leads the nineteen major industrial nations in nitrogen oxide emissions per capita. Oxides of nitrogen are an environmental and health threat. They contribute to the production of acid rain and air pollution, particularly urban smog, as well as lung and other respiratory diseases. Per capita, America releases more than twice the amount of nitrogen oxides as France or the Netherlands, and eight times as much as Japan. Our emissions account for about half of the total among the nineteen major industrial nations.

Acid rain is a very real global problem for the 1990s and beyond. Acidification of the environment changes the pH balance of lakes, threatening fish populations, many of which have already declined in recent decades. On land, "areas of forest soil have increased in acidity by factors of five to ten over the past 20 to 50 years," according to the Organization for Economic Cooperation and Development.[6] Some forests have been decimated as a result. Acid rain is caused primarily by the release of sulfur dioxide, of which the United States is the world's largest producer in absolute terms.[7] We emit more than twenty million tons of sulfur dioxide a year, compared to thirteen million tons a year in China, a nation with four times our population.[8]

Acid rain has gained attention as an environmental hazard because of its transnational effects: sulfur and other pollutants "travel long distances, cross national boundaries, and can have negative impacts on the environment far away from sources."[9] Canada's acid rain problem, for example, is in great part the result of sulfur dioxide emissions in the American Midwest. Scandinavian nations bear the same burden from emissions in neighboring European countries. As a result, there has been agreement internationally on limiting sulfur use and even some progress: sulfur dioxide contributions have decreased between

30 and 75 percent in major industrial nations over the past two decades.[10]

Still, the United States spends less on pollution control as a percentage of public R&D expenditures than Canada, Germany, the U.K., and many other countries.[11]

Tons per capita of carbon dioxide (CO_2) emissions from energy use, 1988; nitrogen oxide (NO_x) emissions, kilograms per capita, 1987:

COUNTRY	CARBON DIOXIDE	NITROGEN OXIDES
United States	**5.8**	**80.4**
Canada	4.8	74.9
Australia	4.3	—
Finland	3.7	56.6
Denmark	3.4	48.5
Netherlands	3.4	37.9
Belgium	3.2	—
Germany	3.2	46.7
United Kingdom	2.9	44.0
Sweden	2.5	37.4
Austria	2.2	—
Ireland	2.2	—
Japan	2.2	9.6
Norway	2.1	53.7
New Zealand	2.0	—
Italy	1.9	27.3
Switzerland	1.9	27.6
France	1.8	31.6
Spain	1.5	—

Source: Organization for Economic Cooperation and Development, *Environmental Indicators* (Paris: OECD, 1991), pp. 17, 23.

- **We're Next to Last in percentage of population "very concerned" about global warming due to carbon dioxide emissions.**

Thirty percent of Americans polled say they are "very concerned" about climate changes, such as global warming, that can occur as a result of carbon dioxide emissions. Only the Belgians, among the nations polled, are less concerned. In Norway, 65 percent of the population—the largest percentage of all nations surveyed—is worried about global warming and other effects carbon dioxide might have on climate.

Percentage of people "very concerned" about "possible climate changes brought about by carbon dioxide," 1988–90:

COUNTRY	PERCENTAGE CONCERNED ABOUT CO_2	COUNTRY	PERCENTAGE CONCERNED ABOUT CO_2
Norway	65	United Kingdom	40
Denmark	54	Netherlands	36
Spain	50	France	34
Germany	48	Ireland	34
Italy	48	**United States**	**30**
Finland	44	Belgium	29
Japan	43		

Source: Organization for Economic Cooperation and Development, *The State of the Environment* (Paris: OECD, 1991), p. 281.

WATER

- **We're Number One in percentage of population with access to safe drinking water.**
- **We're Number One in consumption of beverages other than drinking water.**

The thirst of Americans seems insatiable—except when quenched by Coke or Pepsi. Nearly all U.S. citizens have "reasonable access to a safe and adequate drinking water supply," according to World Priorities.[12] While other countries enjoy similar access to drinking water, only 83 percent of South Koreans, 79 percent of Finns, and 67 percent of Poles have safe water. In Cambodia, as little as 3 percent of the population has access to safe drinking water.[13]

Ironically, commercial beverage intake seems proportional to access to safe water. At the low end are nations whose citizens have no choice but to drink contaminated water. At the other extreme are countries where consumption of coffee, tea, bottled water, milk, juice, and soft drinks is heavy even though clean drinking water is available. "Where tap water is purest and most accessible," writes Alan Durning in *State of the World 1991,* "its use as a beverage is declining. It now typically accounts for only a quarter of drinks in industrial countries."[14] Indeed, in the U.S., tap water consumption has been cut in half in the last twenty years to just 20 percent of all beverage intake. At the same time, soft drink consumption has doubled. The fact that Americans drink more soft drinks than water from the faucet is more than a curiosity. Consumption of individually packaged drinks (whose containers are usually recyclable but are rarely recycled—see below) adds to our waste disposal problem, and the annual cost of 147 gallons of commercial beverage per person is considerable.

Number of eight-ounce servings of Coca-Cola soft drink products consumed per person, 1990:[15]

COUNTRY	SOFT DRINKS PER PERSON	COUNTRY	SOFT DRINKS PER PERSON
United States	**292**	United Kingdom	99
Mexico	263	Philippines	92
Australia	224	Italy	86
Norway	200	South Korea	63
Canada	180	France	48
Germany (unified)	149	Taiwan	48
Spain	148	Thailand	42
Japan	112	Morocco	32
Colombia	111	Turkey	20
Argentina	105	Indonesia	4
Brazil	99		

Source: "For Coke, World Is Its Oyster," *The New York Times*, November 21, 1991, p. D1. Original: company reports.

It's the real thing?

Annual U.S. beverage intake, gallons per capita, 1990 and 1970:

BEVERAGE	1990	1970
Soft drinks	47.5	22.7
Tap water	35.8	68.0
Coffee	25.2	35.7
Beer	23.4	18.5
Milk	19.0	22.8
Tea	7.2	5.2
Bottled water	8.8	—
Juice	6.9	6.5
Powdered drinks	5.3	—
Wine	2.0	1.3
Spirits	1.4	1.8
Total	**182.5**	**182.5**

Source: *Beverage Industry* magazine, vol. 82, no. 2, February 1991, p. 21.

• **We're Number One in use of freshwater resources.**

America withdraws more water annually from its lakes, rivers, and other freshwater bodies than any industrial country. In absolute terms, as a nation we consume 467 cubic *kilometers* of renewable water annually, more than five times that of Japan, a nation with roughly half our population.[16] On average, each American uses nearly 2,000 cubic meters of freshwater per year, seven times as much as the average Briton or Dane. This resource is essential not only for domestic uses, but for agriculture and industry.

Annual withdrawal, in cubic meters, of internal renewable water resources per capita, late 1980s:[17]

COUNTRY	WATER WITHDRAWAL	COUNTRY	WATER WITHDRAWAL
United States	**1,896**	Japan	692
Canada	1,691	New Zealand	571
Australia	1,306	Norway	531
Spain	1,176	Austria	417
Netherlands	980	Sweden	355
Italy	940	United Kingdom	262
Belgium	917	Denmark	254
Finland	809	Ireland	135
France	774	Switzerland	106
Germany	722		

Sources: Organization for Economic Cooperation and Development, *Environmental Indicators* (Paris: OECD, 1991), p. 25; World Resources Institute, *World Resources 1990–91* (New York: Oxford University Press, 1990), pp. 330–31.

CONSUMPTION, WASTE, AND RECYCLING

- **We're Number One in forest depletion.**

Stable forests are essential to most countries' environmental, economic, and social well-being. When most Americans think of deforestation, they think of the loss of rain forests in Brazil and other tropical countries. This concern is well founded: rates of deforestation for some tropical areas are as high as 7 percent *annually*.[18] But, we should not overlook the fact that, among the nineteen major industrial nations, the United States leads in percentage of wooded areas lost during the last two decades. In large part, this is because we lead all countries in the world in production of roundwood (unprocessed wood from forests). "Since 1978 the United States has felled more trees than any other country," says *The Universal Almanac*.[19] Roundwood production in the United States has increased 46 percent since the mid 1970s.[20]

As a result, between 1970 and 1988, we experienced a 3.4 percent depletion of our forests. During this period, only one other major industrial nation, Finland, experienced a decline in forest area, and their loss was a mere 0.1 percent. France, Italy, and Spain increased their forest area substantially, while two "sparsely wooded" countries, the United Kingdom and Ireland, increased their forest area 25.5 percent and 38.4 percent respectively. Increases in these nations were largely due to "an active reforestation policy," according to the OECD's *State of the Environment*.[21] Unfortunately, the quality and diversity of trees planted—essential factors in successful reforestation—cannot be determined from this quantitative data.

Percentage change in forest and other wooded areas, 1970–88:

COUNTRY	PERCENTAGE CHANGE	COUNTRY	PERCENTAGE CHANGE
United States	**−3.4**	Denmark	4.4
Finland	−0.1	Austria	4.5
Japan	0.1	Norway	5.6
Netherlands	0.7	France	8.2
New Zealand	1.3	Spain	8.9
Sweden	1.4	Italy	9.5
Canada	1.6	Australia	13.1
Belgium	1.7	United Kingdom	25.5
Germany	2.7	Ireland	38.4

Source: Organization for Economic Cooperation and Development, *Environmental Indicators* (Paris: OECD, 1991), p. 31.

- **We're Number One in paper consumption per capita.**
- **We're Number One in garbage per capita.**

Each year, the average American uses 700 pounds of paper, more than citizens from any other nation for which data is available (although Sweden is a close second). This may help explain why the United States leads the nineteen major industrial nations in municipal waste generated per person. Americans use 50 percent more paper than the Japanese per capita and almost twice as much as the British. As individual consumers, we produce more than 200 million tons of garbage each year, and our industries produce 760 million tons.[22] Excluding industrial waste, each American produces nearly a ton of garbage a year, more than twice as much per capita as the Swiss and Japanese, and nearly three times as much as the French and Italians. Our municipal waste has increased 33 percent since 1975, while Germany's has increased a minuscule 0.1 percent.[23]

As the politics of disposal heat up, the mountains of waste in the United States are causing a big stink. Mandatory recycling plans are being adopted by local and state governments, but not as thoroughly or quickly as most environmentalists would like. Overflowing landfills leave us with floating barges of garbage in search of disposal sites. And controversial arrangements have been established in which some municipalities, like New York City, pay to have their refuse disposed of in neighboring states, such as New Jersey.

Annual paper consumption in pounds per capita, 1988; and annual municipal waste generation, pounds per capita, late 1980s:

COUNTRY	PAPER CONSUMPTION PER CAPITA (LBS.)	WASTE PER CAPITA (LBS.)
United States	**699**	**1,901**
Australia	342	1,498
New Zealand	345	1,456
Canada	543	1,390
Finland	449	1,338
Norway	333	1,045
Denmark	—	1,032
Netherlands	428	1,027
Switzerland	—	939
Japan	450	867
United Kingdom	360	777
Germany	448	728
Spain	—	708
Sweden	685	697
Belgium	430	689
Ireland	—	684
France	—	667
Italy	—	662
Austria	—	502
Average	—	**979**

Sources: Organization for Economic Cooperation and Development, *Environmental Indicators* (Paris: OECD, 1991), p. 45; Renate Kroesa, "The Greenpeace Guide to Paper" (Vancouver, B.C.: Greenpeace, 1990), p. 41.

- **We're Number One in junk mail.**

Each week, the average American receives about five pieces of third-class mail, including catalogs, advertisements, solicitations, and small parcels better known as "junk mail." Close to 40 percent of all mail is junk mail; 64 billion pieces were recorded in 1990, up from 28 billion in 1979. The majority of it comes to our homes unsolicited and the majority of it is unread when it hits the garbage. Still, more than half of all American adults shop at home (54.4 percent), an increase of 72 percent from 1983 according to the Direct Marketing Association's 1990 figures. The result of all this junk mail is more than $8 billion in revenue for the United States Postal Service and lots of excess paper for the rest of us.

Volume of addressed direct mail, 1987–90:

COUNTRY	MILLION PIECES	PIECES PER CAPITA
United States	**63,700**	**254**
Norway	511	120
Sweden	615	73
Germany	3,357	55
Belgium	533	54
Finland	240	48
Denmark	225	44
France	2,376	43
Netherlands	588	40
United Kingdom	1,626	29
Ireland	20	6

Sources: *European Marketing Data and Statistics 1991* (London: Euromonitor Publications, 1991), p. 322. Original: Services Postaux Europeans. U.S.: Direct Marketing Association (New York, NY).

- **We're Number 14 in recycling paper.**
- **We're Number 16 in recycling glass.**

Our low rate of recycling is particularly deplorable given the volume of garbage we produce. Germany, Japan, Sweden, and Spain recycle one to two thirds more of their paper waste than does the United States. The Netherlands has the best record: they recover 53 percent of their paper and 62 percent of their glass. Glass recycling is also common in Japan and New Zealand. Only 12 percent of our glass is reused; fifteen nations do better.

Percentage of paper and cardboard recycled and percentage of glass recycled, 1980s:

COUNTRY	PAPER RECYCLED[24]	GLASS RECYCLED[25]
Netherlands	53.0	62.0
Japan	49.6	54.4
Spain	44.1	22.0
Germany	41.2	37.0
Sweden	40.0	20.0
Switzerland	38.0	17.0
Austria	36.8	44.0
Belgium	33.0	39.0
Finland	33.0	20.0
France	33.0	26.0
Australia	31.8	17.0
Denmark	31.0	32.0
United Kingdom	30.0	13.0
United States	**29.0**	**12.0**
Norway	27.0	—
Canada	20.0	12.0
New Zealand	19.0	53.0
Ireland	15.0	8.0
Italy	—	38.0

Sources: *The Economist Book of Vital World Statistics* (New York: Times Books, 1990), p. 253; Renate Kroesa, "The Greenpeace Guide to Paper" (Vancouver, B.C.: Greenpeace, 1990), p. 41.

• We're Number One in hazardous waste per capita.

The United States generates 275 million tons of hazardous waste each year, more than one ton per inhabitant. Canada, the next largest producer of hazardous waste in relative terms, generates about one ninth as much waste per capita.

In the United States, opposition to toxic waste disposal grew around toxic dumping scandals like the one at Love Canal near Niagara Falls, New York. Although toxic wastes are supposed to be disposed of in a safe manner, more than twenty thousand

American landfills were deemed potentially hazardous during the mid 1980s.[26] The cost of getting rid of hazardous waste can be quite high: waste with PCBs (polychlorinated biphenyls) can run as much as $4,500 per ton. In all, the United States spent $19 billion on the controlled disposal of hazardous wastes in 1988.[27]

To avoid high costs and the potential danger of hazardous wastes, nations have looked for cheap ways to dispose of toxic material, including dumping it at sea and shipping it to other countries for disposal. Export of hazardous wastes became publicly known in the early 1980s. In 1985, the Organization for Economic Cooperation and Development established guidelines to control "transfrontier movement of waste," including transfers from Western to Eastern European nations, and what it describes as "several 'shady deals' between American and/or European firms and African governments."[28] Germany leads the industrial nations in export of hazardous wastes, with more than a million tons shipped in the most recent year for which data is available.[29]

Annual hazardous waste generation, tons per 100,000 people, late 1980s:

COUNTRY	HAZARDOUS WASTE	COUNTRY	HAZARDOUS WASTE
United States[30]	**110,800**	France	5,300
Canada	12,500	Norway	4,700
Netherlands	10,100	Spain	4,300
Germany	9,800	Austria	2,600
Belgium	9,300	Austrialia	1,800
United Kingdom	7,900	Denmark	1,800
Italy	6,600	New Zealand	1,800
Sweden	6,000	Ireland	600
Switzerland	5,900	Japan[31]	500
Finland	5,400		

Source (for chart and text): Organization for Economic Cooperation and Development, *Environmental Indicators* (Paris: OECD, 1991), p. 45.

NUCLEAR ENERGY

- **We're Number One in nuclear reactors in operation.**
- **We're Number One in nuclear reactors shut down, suspended, or canceled.**

Twenty-five nations now have "installed nuclear capacity," providing for more than four hundred commercial reactors worldwide.[32] More than one hundred of these reactors are in the United States and we generate more nuclear energy annually than any country in the world in absolute terms.[33] France is the most dependent on nuclear energy, deriving 70 percent of its electricity from this source, compared to 20 percent in the United States.[34]

Though nuclear power was originally touted as a cure-all for the world's energy problems, it has been under fire almost since its inception as a commercial form of energy in the 1950s. The controversy over nuclear power has become further embattled due to two recent developments: first, the 1986 Chernobyl reactor accident in the former USSR, which contaminated more than two hundred thousand people and increased public opposition worldwide to nuclear energy; and second, the realization that we need alternatives to fossil fuels (because of global warming), which for some energy experts means more reliance on nuclear energy.[35]

The antinuclear trend seems to be prevailing at the moment, judging by the large number of shut-down, suspended, and canceled reactors in America and throughout the world. The mid 1980s may have been the apex of nuclear power's expansion, as antinuclear advocacy and accidents like the one at Chernobyl subsequently have created an increasingly ambivalent, if not hostile, attitude toward nuclear energy. As a result of public pressure, Italy, the Netherlands, and other nations have delayed plans to expand nuclear power.[36] Still, some nuclear advocates say that improvements can be made to ensure that reactors are safer and less costly to operate.

Number of commercial nuclear reactors in operation in countries with ten or more, as of the end of 1988, and number of reactors shut down, suspended, and canceled, end of 1988:

COUNTRY	OPERABLE REACTORS	INOPERABLE REACTORS
United States	**108**	**52**
Soviet Union	56	5
France	55	5
Japan	38	1
Germany (unified)[37]	28	6
Canada	18	3
Sweden	12	1
Spain	10	4

Source: World Resources Institute, *World Resources 1990–91* (New York: Oxford University Press, 1990), p. 324.

• We're Number One in nuclear testing.

Although international agreements were made as far back as the 1960s to put an end to nuclear testing, the practice has continued. Nuclear devices have been exploded for research purposes in the atmosphere, underwater, and underground. Since the aim of nuclear testing is generally to develop more refined and effective nuclear weapons, it is reasonable to doubt the necessity of the practice in the post–cold war age. The United States is responsible for 951 of the 1,910 nuclear test explosions that have been conducted worldwide since 1945, the largest share of any nation.[38] The Soviet Union has exploded 715 nuclear weapons, though it has now placed a unilateral ban on nuclear testing. The U.S. government spends in excess of $400 million a year on nuclear testing.

Source: "An End to All Nuclear Explosions: The Long-Overdue Test Ban," *The Defense Monitor,* Center for Defense Information, Washington, D.C., 20:1.

GAS AND OIL

- **We're Number One in gasoline consumption per capita.**
- **We're Number One in increase of oil imports.**

The United States leads the world in gasoline consumption per capita because we drive the most and our gasoline prices are among the cheapest. A gallon of gasoline costs $1.07 on average in Los Angeles, compared to $3.69 in Paris, $4.05 in Tokyo, and $4.33 in Milan.[39] America's incessant gas guzzling has also helped make us Number One in increasing reliance on foreign oil.

The oil crisis of the late 1970s convinced many Americans, including some politicians, that the United States needed to free itself from dependence on foreign oil. During the Persian Gulf war of 1991, some said that a sound energy policy, emphasizing domestic alternatives to oil and decreased reliance on oil-producing nations, could have prevented our desert showdown with Saddam Hussein. Between 1982 and 1988, oil imports increased in the United States and *decreased* in Canada, France, Italy, and the United Kingdom. Our increase in oil imports was five times that of Japan and Germany.

**Kilograms of motor gasoline consumed per capita, 1989; and
average annual percentage growth of oil imports, 1982 to 1988:**

COUNTRY	GASOLINE CONSUMED PER CAPITA	GROWTH OF OIL IMPORTS (%)[40]
United States	**1,272**	**7.2**
Canada	947	− 62.1
Australia	741	− 25.0
Switzerland	531	2.0
Sweden	515	− 3.3
New Zealand	485	− 4.4
Germany	456	1.3
Netherlands	437	2.4
Norway	433	− 20.9
United Kingdom	421	− 7.3
Finland	417	0.6
Austria	344	0.7
France	344	− 0.7
Belgium	296	1.1
Denmark	294	− 9.0
Japan	254	1.4
Ireland	236	− 1.5
Italy	229	− 1.0
Spain	195	1.4

Sources: United Nations, *Energy Statistics Yearbook 1989* (New York: United Nations, 1991), pp. 194–207. *World Competitiveness Report 1991*, published by IMD International, Lausanne, Switzerland, and World Economic Forum, Geneva, Switzerland, p. 287.

> ### • We're Number One in major oil spills affecting our shores.
>
> American shores have been subjected to more major oil spills than those of any other country in the world.[41] Between 1967 and 1989 there were seventeen major oil spills in U.S. waters. During the same period, there were six spills on the coasts of France and the United Kingdom, and four affecting Canada, Japan, Spain, and South Africa. In 1989, the *Exxon Valdez* spilled 35 tons of oil off the coast of Alaska, killing wildlife and requiring an enormous cleanup effort. The *Valdez* spill was not the largest in U.S. history; a 1975 Delaware spill and a 1979 Texas spill each released 40 tons of oil into the sea. The largest spill during the period in question occurred in 1979 when the Greek *Atlantic Express* accidentally discharged 276 tons (more than seven times the amount of the *Valdez*) near the Caribbean island of Tobago.
>
> Source: Organization for Economic Cooperation and Development, *The State of the Environment* (Paris: OECD, 1991), pp. 75–76.

CARS, ROADS, AND RAILWAYS

• We're Number One in cars per capita.
• We're Number One in using cars rather than public transportation.

Public transportation in the United States is something of an oxymoron, considering that only 3 percent of the public's trips are made by bus, train, ferry, etc. Americans would rather drive! Our zeal to be behind the wheel also makes us the leader, per capita, in cars owned, road travel, and spending on personal transportation.

There are more than 130 million cars in the United States, and the average American drives 8,260 miles per year, twice as much as the average German and three times as much as the average Japanese citizen. The French and Swedes, who are more than three times as likely to use public transportation as Americans, spend half as much as we do on personal transportation. Other nations are gaining ground, though. Japan experienced the largest growth in the use of cars—251 percent—between 1970 and 1988.[42]

Percentage of urban passenger trips made by automobile or public transportation, selected countries, 1978–87:[43]

COUNTRY	AUTO	PUBLIC TRANSPORTATION
Soviet Union	12	88
Poland	15	85
Hungary	11	58
Czechoslovakia	13	52
East Germany	24	27
United Kingdom	45	19
Sweden	36	11
France	47	11
Germany	48	11
Netherlands	45	5
United States	**82**	**3**

Source: John Pucher, "Capitalism, Socialism, and Urban Transportation: Policies and Travel Behavior in the East and West," *Journal of the American Planning Association,* Summer 1990.

Passenger cars in use per 100 persons, 1989; and vehicle miles traveled per capita annually, 1989:

COUNTRY	CARS PER 100 PERSONS	MILES TRAVELED PER CAPITA
United States	**58**	**8,260**
New Zealand	51	4,120
Germany	49	4,342
Canada	47	5,302
Australia	46	5,766
Italy	46	3,199
France	41	4,584
Austria	38	4,413
Finland	38	4,871
Norway	38	3,098
United Kingdom	38	3,881
Belgium	37	3,261
Netherlands	36	3,731
Denmark	32	4,351
Spain	29	1,573
Japan	27	2,621
Ireland	22	4,062

Source: Organization for Economic Cooperation and Development, *Environmental Indicators* (Paris: OECD, 1991), p. 61.

- **We're Number One in length of railroad network.**
- **We're Number 18 in passenger usage of railroads.**

The American railroad system boasts about 140,000 miles of track, more than six times as much as France, the country with the second largest rail network among the nineteen major industrial nations. But despite its smaller size, population, and railroad length, France's trains log three times as many passenger kilometers in *absolute* terms as U.S. trains. On a per capita basis, only the Australians travel less by train than we do.

The Japanese travel by rail the most: 1,712 miles a year per person, thirty-five times the distance traveled by the average American. The Swiss travel amost twenty times as much on trains as we do on average. There is a simple explanation for these huge discrepancies: Americans continue to drive private vehicles at the expense of taking public transportation.

Passenger miles traveled by rail annually, per capita, 1986–87:

COUNTRY[44]	MILES	COUNTRY	MILES
Japan	1,712	Finland	385
Switzerland	944	United Kingdom	359
France	660	Norway	323
Austria	601	Spain	244
Denmark	582	Ireland	212
Germany (unified)	493	New Zealand	74
Italy	450	Canada	49
Sweden	444	**United States**	**48**
Belgium	397	Australia	34
Netherlands	388		

Sources: *European Marketing Data and Statistics 1991* (London: Euromonitor Publications, 1991), pp. 416–417; *International Marketing Data and Statistics 1991* (London: Euromonitor Publications, 1991), pp. 538–43. Original: United Nations/Union Internationale des Chemins de Fer (UIC).

FAX AT OUR FINGERTIPS

MEDIA, ARTS, AND TECHNOLOGY

Marshall McLuhan's aphorism, "the medium is the message," may sound trite, but it is an accurate description of how we live today. Industrial and developing nations alike are increasingly slaves to information and technology. While members of the media once roamed the globe seeking important events to report, the events now seek media coverage in order to establish their importance. Leaders of warring nations communicate live by satellite, demonstrations begin when the cameras arrive and end when they are whisked away, struggling revolutionary movements fax their pleas for help to the world.

The information age in America has brought with it an increasing unfamiliarity with the printed word. Television, computers, and other forms of electronic communication are on the rise, while newspapers and books are becoming increasingly outdated and scarce. This transition is startling for many Americans, most of whom still cannot program their videocassette recorders let alone take advantage of state-of-the-art multimedia technology.

DAILY NEWS

- **We're Number One in televisions and radios per capita.**
- **We're Number 18 in daily newspaper circulation per capita.**

Ours is an audio-visual culture and newspapers are paying the price. The United States boasts 812 televisions and 2,120 radios per 1,000 inhabitants, or nearly one television and more than two radios per person. Ninety-eight percent of American households own at least one television set, only 2 percent of which are black and white, according to Nielsen. Sixty-four percent of American households own more than two TVs, and sixty percent of us have cable television.[1]

America's reliance on electronic media, particularly television, for information has led to a decline in readership of daily newspapers. While the United States publishes 1,611 daily newspapers (second only to India, which publishes nearly two thousand), circulation of dailies is higher in seventeen other countries. The former East Germany's newspaper circulation is the largest per person in the world, almost double that of the United States.[2] Japan's newspaper readership per capita is the second highest in the world; in fact, their total circulation of newspapers is larger than ours despite the fact that the American population is about twice that of Japan.

Nations with higher daily newspaper circulation per capita than the United States. Figures for newspapers, television, and radio are per 1,000 inhabitants, 1988:[3]

COUNTRY	NEWSPAPER	TELEVISION	RADIO
East Germany	585	759	669
Japan	566	589	863
Finland	551	486	997
Norway	551	350	795
Sweden	526	395	875
Switzerland	504	408	401
Soviet Union	474	319	686
United Kingdom	421	435	1146
Austria	362	487	627
Denmark	359	526	879
West Germany	347	379	956
Czechoslovakia	345	395	274
New Zealand	327	372	917
Netherlands	314	478	912
Singapore	289	360	307
Bulgaria	267	189	224
Hungary	273	404	590
United States	**251**	**812**	**2120**

Sources: UNESCO, *Statistical Yearbook 1990* (Paris: UNESCO, 1990), Tables 7.16, 10.1, and 10.2.

BIG SCREENS, LITTLE SCREENS

- **We're Number One in time spent watching television.**

Americans spend almost thirty hours a week watching television, the most of any nation for which data is available. Japan and the United Kingdom are close behind, while the Scandinavian nations watch the least. In the United States, women over fifty-five watch the most television per week (40 hours and 48 minutes), while men age 18 to 24 watch the least (20 hours and 50 minutes). In individual time slots, women over fifty-five generally watch the most, except between 7:00 A.M. and 1:00 P.M. on Saturday, when children age 2 to 5 watch twice as much as adults.[4]

Hours and minutes spent watching television, per week, 1990:[5]

COUNTRY	TV WATCHING	COUNTRY	TV WATCHING
United States	**29:05**	Denmark	17:33
Japan	28:28	Ireland	16:55
United Kingdom	25:35	Netherlands	16:48
France	20:54	Switzerland	15:25
Belgium	20:08	Sweden	15:01
Austria	19:24	Norway	14:22
Germany	19:15	Finland	12:28

Source: A. C. Nielsen Co. (Northbrook, Ill.).

- **We're Number One in percentage of homes with VCRs.**
- **We're Number 11 in cinema attendance.**

Videocassette recorders have quickly made the transition from novelty to necessity, not only in the United States, but in most major industrial nations and even in many developing ones. In 1978, 400,000 VCRs were sold in America. Now, more than ten million units are sold each year. Industry analysts estimate that three quarters of American households are equipped with VCRs, the largest share of any of the nineteen major industrial nations.[6] One corollary result is that "couch potato" has supplanted "yuppie" as the favorite term in our pop psychology lexicon.

The consequences for the silver screen? While big profits are reaped from video release of films, some motion picture industry heads say they are feeling the pain. Americans see more films each year than their counterparts in the nineteen major industrial nations, but ten nations worldwide have higher cinema attendance rates than the United States. Residents of the former Soviet Union are bigger filmgoers by far: they see three times as many movies on average as we do and lead all nations for which information is available. Residents of other Eastern European nations also go to the movies more often than Americans, as do citizens in Hong Kong, Singapore, North Korea, Vietnam, and India (where the most films are produced as well: in 1987, 806 full-length features were made in India compared to 578 in the U.S.).[7] In fact, the average number of cinema attendances per year in all industrial countries is 5.6 per year, compared to 4.5 per year in the United States.[8] Between our televisions, videocassette recorders, cable hookups, and satellite dishes, it's impressive that we make it out of the house as often as we do.

Percentage of households with videocassette recorders, 1988–91:[9]

COUNTRY	VCRS	COUNTRY	VCRS
United States	**74**	Denmark	40
Australia	66	Ireland	40
Canada	65	Switzerland	40
New Zealand	63	Austria	37
United Kingdom	56	Finland	37
Japan	55	Belgium	35
Norway	48	Spain	34
Netherlands	46	France	30
Sweden	46	Italy	20
Germany	41		

Sources: *European Marketing Data and Statistics 1991* (London: Euromonitor Publications, 1991), p. 323; *International Marketing Data and Statistics 1991* (London: Euromonitor Publications, 1991), p. 411.

Annual cinema attendances per person, 1986–88:[10]

COUNTRY	FILMS ATTENDED	COUNTRY	FILMS ATTENDED
Soviet Union	13.6	France	2.5
Singapore	12.5	Switzerland	2.5
Hong Kong	12.3	Denmark	2.2
Bulgaria	9.5	Spain	2.2
North Korea	9.2	Sweden	2.2
Romania	9.1	Italy	1.9
India	5.9	Germany[11]	1.8
Vietnam	5.8	Belgium	1.6
Hungary	5.3	Austria	1.5
Czechoslovakia	4.8	Finland	1.3
United States	**4.5**	United Kingdom	1.3
Ireland	3.3	Japan	1.2
Canada	3.0	Netherlands	1.1
Norway	3.0		

Source: UNESCO, *Statistical Yearbook 1990* (Paris: UNESCO, 1990), Table 9.3.

THE PRINTED WORD

• **We're Last in book titles published per capita.**

The printed word was once considered a repository for a culture's wisdom and beauty. Is the United States losing that source compared to other nations? About fifty thousand books are published each year in the United States, yet relative to the size of our population we produce fewer new titles annually than all industrial nations for which data is available, including Romania and Albania.

Americans spend about $18 billion a year to buy roughly 2.2 billion books (about nine per capita), more than half of which are softbound volumes.[12] Denmark spends the most on books, 35 percent more than Americans in real expenditures per capita; Germany, the United Kingdom, France, Ireland, and Japan also spend more on books.[13] Denmark's citizens are also the most plentiful book publishers, with about 22 new works published per 10,000 people each year. By comparison, the United States publishes 1.8 new books per 10,000 people, less than a tenth of the Danish figure. A factor to consider in this comparison is the large size of the American population, but Japan produces twice as many books per capita as the United States with half our population—in other words, about the same number of new titles annually. And the Soviet Union, with a larger population than the United States, publishes 60 percent more books per capita.

We're Number One!

Book titles published per 10,000 persons, 1986–88:

COUNTRY	TITLES PER 10,000 PERSONS	COUNTRY	TITLES PER 10,000 PERSONS
Denmark	21.6	Portugal	7.5
Switzerland	18.8	Ireland	7.2
Finland	18.3	Czechoslovakia	6.7
Norway	16.0	Bulgaria	5.1
Sweden	13.6	Israel	4.8
Austria	11.7	Greece	4.6
Spain	9.8	Japan	3.6
Germany	9.3	Albania	3.0
United Kingdom	9.2	Italy	3.0
Netherlands	8.9	Soviet Union	2.9
Hungary	8.6	Poland	2.7
Belgium	8.5	Romania	2.3
France	7.7	**United States**	**1.8**

Sources: United Nations Development Programme, *Human Development Report 1991* (New York: Oxford University Press, 1991), p. 182; UNESCO, *Statistical Yearbook 1990* (Paris: UNESCO, 1990) Table 7.4.

• We're Last in dissemination of deep thinking.

The fact that the United States is last in new book titles per capita would not be so ominous if there were signs that America was reading works of substance, something in addition to trashy romance novels and cheesy spy thrillers. One indicator we might use to compare the "seriousness" or "thoughtfulness" of what we read in America to that of other nations is the number of philosophy titles published annually. By this standard, we disseminate less deep thinking than any other industrial nation for which data is available. Japan publishes four times as many philosophy volumes per capita as the United States, and Germany publishes more than ten times as many. Denmark—the leader in yet another literary category—publishes 80 philosophy books per 1 million population annually, while the U.S. publishes 3 philosophy titles per 1 million.[14]

Source: *European Marketing Data and Statistics 1991* (London: Euromonitor Publications, 1991), p. 446. Original: UNESCO, *Statistical Yearbook 1990* (Paris: UNESCO, 1990), Table 7.5.

• **We're Number 13 in library books per person.**

Twelve nations boast more library books per capita than the
United States, including many of the same nations that publish
more new titles per capita than we do—Romania, Poland, Bulgaria, the former Soviet Union, etc. The Scandinavian nations
also fare well in this category. Sweden has the most library
books, 12.9 per person, more than twice that of the United
States.

Library books per person, 1986–88:

COUNTRY	LIBRARY BOOKS PER PERSON	COUNTRY	LIBRARY BOOKS PER PERSON
Sweden	12.9	**United States**	**5.8**
Bulgaria	10.8	Canada	5.6
Finland	10.7	Netherlands	5.4
Norway	9.4	Belgium	5.0
Soviet Union	9.5	Germany	4.1
Denmark	9.1	Switzerland	3.7
Poland	9.1	New Zealand	3.1
Hungary	8.7	United Kingdom	3.1
Romania	8.0	France	1.7
Austria	7.6	Australia	1.5
Japan	6.1	Spain	1.3
Czechoslovakia	6.0	Italy	0.6

Sources: United Nations Development Programme, *Human Development Report 1991* (New York:
Oxford University Press, 1991), p. 182; UNESCO, *Statistical Yearbook 1990* (Paris: UNESCO, 1990),
Table 7.1.

CULTURE HIGH AND LOW

- **We're Number One in museums.**

Spain has the Prado, France the Louvre, and Italy the Uffizi, but citizens of the nations with the world's most celebrated museums attend them quite infrequently. The average Frenchman makes 0.2 museum visits per year; in other words, one visit every five years. By the same comparison, the average Italian goes to a museum once every ten years. Perhaps the locals don't want to contend with all the foreign tourists who flock to the great halls.

The Scandinavian and Eastern European countries have relatively high museum attendance rates, with Denmark and Bulgaria sharing top honors. Americans rate a fairly average 1.4 museum visits annually, although we do have the most museums of any nation for which information is available. Germany, Canada, the former Soviet Union, and France have between 1,200 and 3,000 museums, while the United States has more than 7,000.

Annual number of museum attendances per person and number of museums, 1984–87:[15]

COUNTRY	ATTENDANCES	NUMBER OF MUSEUMS
Bulgaria	1.7	206
Denmark	1.7	280
Austria	1.6	179
Hungary	1.5	541
Israel	1.5	95
United States[16]	**1.4**	**7,431**
Sweden	1.4	167
Switzerland	1.4	620
Germany (unified)	1.3	2,998
Norway	1.2	421
Netherlands	1.1	548
Canada	0.9	1,237
Japan	0.8	—
Finland	0.6	572
Soviet Union	0.6	1,479
Spain	0.4	—
Australia	0.3	—
France	0.2	1,200
Ireland	0.2	—
Italy	0.1	309
New Zealand	0.1	98

Sources: United Nations Development Programme, *Human Development Report 1991* (New York: Oxford University Press, 1991), p. 182; UNESCO, *Statistical Yearbook 1990* (Paris: UNESCO, 1990), Table 8.1.

• We're Number One in spending on advertising per capita.

The United States spends nearly $130 billion each year just trying to convince itself what to eat, smoke, drink, drive, and wear. That's almost as much as we spend *in toto* on higher education in America each year.[17] In per capita terms, the United States is Number One, spending more than $500 per person annually, twice as much as Japan and Australia, and three times as much as Germany and Denmark.

One of the biggest advertisers in America is Phillip Morris, the cigarette and food company, with more than $2 billion annual spending on advertising—almost three times as much as McDonald's and more than five times as much as Coca-Cola. The U.S. government spends $300 million a year on advertising, much of it for the military.[18]

Total spending on advertising and spending per capita, 1988–90:

COUNTRY	MILLIONS	PER CAPITA
United States	**$128,640**	**$514**
Finland	1,776	359
Switzerland	2,001	302
Canada	6,440	248
Australia	3,928	238
Japan	27,345	223
United Kingdom	11,737	206
Sweden	1,646	195
Norway	759	181
New Zealand	569	173
Germany	10,326	169
Denmark	822	160
Spain	5,967	153
Netherlands	2,198	149
France	8,029	144
Austria	872	115
Belgium	1,095	110
Italy	5,776	101
Ireland	272	77

Sources: *European Marketing Data and Statistics 1991* (London: Euromonitor Publications, 1991), p. 314. *International Marketing Data and Statistics 1991* (London: Euromonitor Publications, 1991), p. 410; U.S.: *Advertising Age*, January 6, 1992, p. S11. Original: Robert Jay Coen, McAnn-Erickson.

CONCLUSION

American pride, even when it is justified, has a tendency to become excessive, slipping into hubris. The Greek root of hubris means "violence," a significant point when one considers the possible results of overblown American pride: from complacency and arrogance to blindness toward our own problems, negligence, and ultimately self-destruction. Richard Lamm, former governor of Colorado, recalls the story of the *Titanic* crew member who boldly told a reporter before the doomed ship set sail: "Mister, even God Almighty couldn't sink this ship."[1] Are we that arrogant? Is the United States heading in the same direction as the *Titanic*?

Humans are by nature competitive animals; because we will always be eager to keep up with the Joneses (whether they live across the street or halfway around the world), it is important that we remember that being Number One has its ups and downs.

Yet, international comparisons are anachronistic in this period of rapid globalization. As the boundaries of nations become increasingly permeable to the exchange of people, goods, and ideas, exclaiming "We're Number One!" may be a very backward way of looking at our world. This book was written not only to point out where we really are Number One, but to show how bankrupt the concept of "me-firstism" really is. Ideally, we should be striving not only to make our nation Number One, but working to ensure that all citizens of the world are Number One—in health care, education, housing, environmental protection, security, freedom, and democracy.

NOTES

INTRODUCTION

1. *The New York Times,* January 14, 1992, p. A19; and September 22, 1991, section 4, p. 2; *Money,* October 1991.

AUTHOR'S NOTE

1. Some sources advise that cross-national comparisons should be made "with caution," as data collection methods may vary from country to country.

2. The World Values Survey is an indispensable source of international opinion data. The survey is a unique academic project that is utilized by many scholars. It takes years to compile, as hundreds of questions are asked of thousands of respondents in scores of nations. As a result, the World Values Survey data used in this book, gathered between 1981 and 1983, are the most recent available. An updated World Values Survey is now being conducted, but data will not be available before 1993. The following additional statement was provided by Professor Ronald Inglehart, who graciously provided tabulated data for the book: "This book uses data from the 1981 World Values Survey, which originated as the European Value Systems Survey, directed by Jan Kerkhofs and Ruud de Moor; it evoked such widespread interest that it was replicated in numerous additional countries around the world. Reports of its findings have been published in many languages; in English, see Stephen Harding, David Phillips and Michael Fogarty, *Contrasting Values in Western Europe* (London: Macmillan, 1986); and Ronald Inglehart, *Culture Shift in Advanced Industrial Society* (Princeton: Princeton University Press, 1990). These data were furnished by Ronald Inglehart of the Institute for Social Research, University of Michigan."

CHRONIC DISORDER: HEALTH AND MEDICAL CARE

1. Robert J. Blendon, Robert Leitman, Ian Morrison, and Karen Donelan, "Satisfaction with Health Systems in Ten Nations," *Health Affairs,* Summer 1990, p. 187.

2. National Center for Health Statistics, *Health, United States, 1990* (Hyattsville, Md.: Public Health Service, 1991), p. 123; and "Children in Peril," *Newsweek,* special issue, summer 1991, p. 18.

3. Geraldine Dallek, "Health-care System Will Continue to Die—Until More Feel the Pain," *Los Angeles Times,* August 19, 1990, Part M, page 5.

4. Developed and developing nations denote the wealthier and poorer nations of the world respectively. The terms "first world" and "third world," or "industrialized" and "nonindustrialized," may be more familiar or preferable to others.

5. Most developed nations refers to members of the Organization for Economic Cooperation and Development.

6. Rates for black Americans are 1990 projections from the U.S. Bureau of the Census, *Statistical Abstract of the United States 1991* (Washington, D.C.: USGPO, 1991), p. 73. Rates for other nations are from 1989, UNICEF, *State of the World's Children 1991* (New York: Oxford University Press, 1991), p. 103.

7. Christine Gorman, "Why Do Blacks Die Young?" *Time,* September 16, 1991, p. 52.

8. U.S. Bureau of the Census, *Statistical Abstract of the United States 1991* (Washington, D.C.: USGPO, 1991), p. 73.

9. Unless otherwise specified, all references to Germany throughout the book include data from the former Federal Republic of Germany (West Germany) only. Data on the former German Democratic Republic (East Germany) is included where it is available and relevant; in such cases, the nations are separately listed using their former names.

10. Organization for Economic Cooperation and Development, *Health Care Systems in Transition* (Paris: OECD, 1990), pp. 11, 116. Industrial nations mentioned here refer to members of the Organization for Economic Cooperation and Development.

11. Fourteen percent of American household expenditures goes to medical care, according to the World Bank, *World Development Report 1991* (Washington, D.C.: Oxford University Press, 1991), p. 223. Figures ranged from 5 percent in Canada to 8 percent in the U.K. to 13 percent in France and Germany. Switzerland's 15 percent figure is excluded here because it refers to a different time period.

12. Organization for Economic Cooperation and Development, *Health Care Systems in Transition* (Paris: OECD, 1990), p. 80.

13. Other contributing factors include the lack of regulation over the cost of new medical technology, a larger number of medical specialists than in other

nations, higher rates of diagnostic tests and surgery, and the medical malpractice crisis. Source: Democratic Study Group, "Why Conservatives Don't Talk About America's Health System," Special Report, No. 102–6, May 24, 1991.

14. Organization for Economic Cooperation and Development, *Health Care Systems in Transition* (Paris: OECD, 1990), p. 116. The original reference made by Jack A. Meyer is to D. Himmelstein and S. Woolhandler, "Cost without benefit," *New England Journal of Medicine,* 314(7):441, 1986; Canada figure is from Democratic Study Group, "Why Conservatives Don't Talk About America's Health System," Special Report, No. 102–6, May 24, 1991, p. 32.

15. "Demands to Fix U.S. Health Care Reach a Crescendo," *The New York Times,* May 19, 1991, section 4, p. 1.

16. Robert J. Blendon et al., "Satisfaction with Health Systems in Ten Nations," *Health Affairs,* Summer 1990, p. 191.

17. "Demands to Fix U.S. Health Care Reach a Crescendo," *The New York Times,* May 19, 1991, section 4, p. 1.

18. Timothy Egan, "Hawaii Shows It Can Offer Health Insurance for All," *The New York Times,* July 23, 1991, p. A1.

19. "Harper's Index," *Harper's Magazine,* October 1988, p. 15.

20. Seventy-three percent say government should spend more on health care. Source: George Gallup, Jr., *The Gallup Poll: Public Opinion 1989* (Wilmington, Del.: Scholarly Resources, 1990), p. 169.

21. Medicare (12.6 percent), Medicaid (6.2 percent), military/veterans' benefits (2.6 percent) as of 1989. Source: National Center for Health Statistics, *Advance Data,* No. 201, June 18, 1991.

22. In addition, many who qualify for Medicare supplement their coverage with private insurance.

23. The U.S. Census Bureau's latest figures show 33.9 million Americans uninsured (13.9 percent of the population) and 63 million without health insurance for at least a month during the previous twenty-eight months. Twenty to fifty million more Americans are underinsured (*Harvard Community Health Plan Annual Report 1990* [Brookline, Mass: Harvard Community Health Plan, 1991], p. 23).

24. Steffie Woolhandler, "A Failing System of Health Care," *Harvard Community Health Plan Annual Report 1990* (Brookline, Mass: Harvard Community Health Plan, 1991), p. 23.

25. Dr. C. Arden Miller at UNC Chapel Hill says his research shows that the Netherlands has 100 percent public health coverage. The OECD's figure is substantially lower (69 percent). The OECD's figure for the U.S. (44 percent) is substantially higher than that given by the U.S. Department of Health's National Center for Health Statistics.

26. U.S. House of Representatives Select Committee on Children, Youth, and Families.

27. Survey information provided by Robert Half International (Menlo Park, Calif.).

28. Mary Wendy Roberts, "What's Bush's Problem With Family Leave?" *The New York Times,* August 30, 1991, p. A23.

29. George Gallup, Jr., *The Gallup Poll: Public Opinion 1990* (Wilmington, Del.: Scholarly Resources, 1991), p. 67.

30. Statistics are for married women age 15 to 44, including some who may be sterile, pregnant, or trying to get pregnant. International statistics regarding male contraceptive usage are not available.

31. Elise F. Jones et al., *Pregnancy, Contraception, and Family Planning Services in Industrialized Countries: A Study of the Alan Guttmacher Institute* (New Haven: Yale University Press, 1989).

32. Alan Guttmacher Institute, *Facts in Brief: Abortion in the United States* (New York: AGI, 1991).

33. In some cases, age groups vary (e.g., 18 to 49); contraception figures are 1975 for Denmark, 1976 for New Zealand, 1977 for Finland, and 1979 for Italy. Abortion statistics are somewhat incomplete for France, Germany, Ireland, Italy, and Japan.

34. For percentage of abortions: U.K. figure is England and Wales; Switzerland is 1984 data; Belgium is 1985 data.

35. England and Wales.

36. International Association for the Evaluation of Educational Achievement, *Science Achievement in Seventeen Countries, A Preliminary Report* (Oxford: Pergamon Press, 1988).

37. Elise F. Jones et al., *Teenage Pregnancy in Industrialized Countries. A Study Sponsored by the Alan Guttmacher Institute* (New Haven: Yale University Press, 1986), p. 215.

38. Alan Guttmacher Institute press release.

39. Ibid.

40. England and Wales.

41. Infant mortality is defined as deaths under one year of age. Though the U.S. appears in the chart to be tied with Belgium, Italy, and New Zealand, these figures are rounded. The Organization for Economic Cooperation and Development's most recent figures are: U.S., 10 per 1,000; Belgium, 9.7; Italy, 9.6; and New Zealand, 9.8, in *Health Care Systems in Transition* (Paris: OECD, 1990), p. 193.

42. Representative George Miller, "Child Health: Lessons from Developed Nations," hearing of the U.S. House of Representatives Select Committee on Children, Youth and Families, March 20, 1990.

43. Children's Defense Fund, *The State of America's Children, 1991* (Washington, D.C.: CDF, 1991), p. 5.

44. National Center for Health Statistics, *Health, United States, 1990* (Hyattsville, Md.: Public Health Service, 1991), p. 9.

45. Christine Gorman, "Why Do Blacks Die Young?" *Time*, September 16, 1991, p. 51.

46. Saudi Arabia is Riyadh only; Jordan, Australia, and Switzerland are 1979. Italy figure (1973) excluded. While Spain's figure is included, it is curiously low and has raised some legitimate doubts. Published by UNICEF, the figure has also been used by the Children's Defense Fund, but the World Bank's *World Development Report* (New York: Oxford University Press, 1991), p. 259, and *World Resources 1990–91* (New York: Oxford University Press, 1991), p. 263, omitted the figure from reports in which they used UNICEF data for other nations.

47. American Academy of Pediatrics, "Immunizations," press release.

48. Children's Defense Fund, *The State of America's Children 1991* (Washington, D.C.: CDF, 1991), p. 6.

49. "President Defers Action on a Plan to Buy and Distribute Vaccines," *The New York Times*, June 23, 1991, p. 1.

50. Rates are for one- to four-year-olds in the U.S., one- to three-year-olds in Europe. In 1985, the federal government suspended funds used to track rates of immunization, so it is difficult to obtain exact figures on how many of our nation's children are at risk of contracting polio, measles, whooping cough, and other childhood diseases. One immunization expert believes that the rates are now lower than the 1985 figures in the chart above (op. cit., Williams, "Immunization"). One problem is that some statistics from the latest U.S. immunization study (1985) are misleading. For example, while it seems that 95 percent of one-year-olds *and* school-age children are fully immunized against polio, the U.S. Department of Health and Human Services correctly notes that only 55 percent of children age *one to four* are immunized. The difference of forty percentage points is best explained by a substantial decrease in the number of children who continue to receive immunization against polio after the age of one, and then an increase at age five or six, when immunization is required for a child to start school. The same pattern appears for measles, rubella, DTP, and mumps vaccines. The problem is that the intervening years, from age two to five, are "when protection is most crucial," according to the American Academy of Pediatrics. The most revealing cross-national comparisons are made, therefore, between immunization rates for preschoolers in different nations.

51. Rate is for combined diphtheria, tetanus, and polio immunizations. Pertussis immunization rate is 89 percent.

52. Figures given in chart are the lower of two available figures. Some cantons have rates as high as 98 percent for polio, 98 percent for DTP, and 70 percent for measles.

53. England and Wales.

54. Still, the figures presented in the chart below provide an accurate *comparative* picture of AIDS prevalence in different nations since the inception of the disease.

55. Gina Kolata, "10 Years of AIDS Battle: Hopes for Success Dim," *The New York Times,* June 3, 1991, p. A14.

56. Centers for Disease Control, personal communication.

57. Figures are through October 1, 1991, for all countries except the U.S., where figures are current through November 1991. Note: AIDS annual figures are updated by WHO retroactively, so 1991 figures are provisional.

58. Japan is excluded on the grounds that only a few hundred AIDS cases have been reported there (see previous chart). While their ignorance cannot be excused, their exposure to AIDS is not comparable to that of other industrialized nations, especially the United States, which has had 270 times as many AIDS cases per capita as Japan. Even Finland, the major industrial nation with the next fewest AIDS cases per capita, has had six times as many cases per capita as Japan. For posterity's sake, 26 percent of the Japanese respondents say coughing or sneezing is a likely transmission mode of AIDS, and 68 percent say they would not work alongside someone with AIDS.

59. Not including carcinoma in situ and nonmelanoma skin cancers, of which there are 100,000 annual cases and 600,000 annual cases respectively. Source: Catherine C. Boring, Teresa S. Squires, Tony Tong, "Cancer Statistics, 1991," *Ca-A Cancer Journal for Clinicians,* vol. 41, no. 1, January/February 1991, p. 28.

60. Author's interview.

61. Data was collected in most countries at multiple sites and not averaged. Consequently, the low and high figures provided represent the range of incidence. In the U.S., figures for whites and blacks were provided separately. A single figure is provided in the cases in which a country reported from only one site.

62. Figures for Pacific Polynesian Islanders (45.95 percent for males; 40.85 percent for females) excluded due to incomplete data.

63. Democratic Study Group, "Why Conservatives Don't Talk About America's Health System," Special Report, No. 102–6, May 24, 1991, p. 51.

64. Data was collected in most countries at multiple sites and not averaged. Consequently, the low and high figures provided represent the range of incidence. In the U.S., figures are generally for white women only. Incidence of breast cancer is significantly lower for black, Latino, and Asian women in the U.S. (with the exception of Hawaiian women, whose rate of 10.87 percent is the highest in the nation). A single figure is provided in the cases in which a country reported from only one site. Also: Spain's death rate figure is 1986.

65. Author's interview.

66. Sources: Eric J. Slora and Martin L. Gonzalez, "Medical Professional Liability Claims and Premiums," in *Socioeconomic Characteristics of Medical Practice 1990/1991,* (Chicago: AMA, 1991), pp. 15–19; "Malpractice Costs Cut Ranks of Obstetricians," *The New York Times,* October 12, 1989, p. A22; Patricia M. Danzon, "The 'Crisis' in Medical Malpractice: A Comparison of

Trends in the United States, Canada, the United Kingdom and Australia," *Law, Medicine & Health Care,* vol. 18: 1–2, Spring–Summer 1990, pp. 48–58. The AMA source reports a lower claim frequency figure and a decrease in claim frequency between 1985 and 1989. Danzon notes that claim frequency appears to have risen since 1989.

67. "Malpractice Costs Cut Ranks of Obstetricians," *The New York Times,* October 12, 1989, p. A22.

68. Quoted in Walter K. Olson, *The Litigation Explosion* (New York: Truman Talley, 1991), p. 6.

69. England and Wales.

70. Only Argentina and Uruguay—steak capitals of the world—eat more beef per capita.

71. Democratic Study Group, "Why Conservatives Don't Talk About America's Health System," Special Report, No. 102–6, May 24, 1991, p. 46.

72. Beef figures include veal, except for Japan.

73. National Center for Health Statistics, *Health, United States, 1990* (Hyattsville, Md.: Public Health Service, 1991), pp. 132–33.

74. Sweden, 1983; Italy, 1981; France, 1979.

75. National Center for Health Statistics, *Health, United States, 1990* (Hyattsville, Md.: Public Health Service, 1991), pp. 137–38.

PIETIES AND PRIORITIES: FAMILY, RELIGION, SEX, SPORTS, AND VICE

1. Survey Research Consultants International, *Index to International Public Opinion, 1988–89* (New York: Greenwood Press, 1990), p. 651.

2. World Values Survey.

3. Doug Bandow, "Home Alone: Should Congress Play With Family Leave?" *Business and Society Review,* spring 1991, p. 41.

4. World Values Survey.

5. Barbara Berliner, *The Book of Answers* (New York: Prentice-Hall, 1990), p. 19.

6. Study: American Psychological Association press release, August 18, 1991. Children involved in divorce: U.S. House of Representatives Select Committee on Children, Youth and Families, "Children's Well-Being: An International Comparison" (Washington, D.C.: USGPO, 1990), p. 35.

7. Joseph S. Nye, Jr., *Bound to Lead: The Changing Nature of American Power* (New York: Basic Books, 1990), p. 203.

8. Australia, France, 1987; Belgium, 1986.

9. A dependent child is defined as under age 18 in the U.S.; ages vary in different nations, from 15 in Ireland to 25 in France. For U.S. statistics, single-parent families may include those living as part of a larger household as well as unmarried couples who cohabitate. Standards vary slightly from country to country.

10. Children's Defense Fund, *The State of America's Children, 1991* (Washington, D.C.: CDF, 1991), p. 2.

11. Britain.

12. Gorton Carruth and Eugene Ehrlich, *The Harper Book of American Quotations* (New York: Harper & Row, 1988), p. 89.

13. More recent (1988–89) figures are available for Canada and the U.S. Ninety-four percent of Americans and Canadians say they would welcome more emphasis on "traditional family ties"; 89 percent of Americans and 88 percent of Canadians say they would welcome more respect for authority.

14. Britain.

15. Woody Allen, "Selections from the Allen Notebooks," in *Without Feathers,* 1975, quoted in Gorton Carruth and Eugene Ehrlich, *The Harper Book of American Quotations* (New York: Harper & Row, 1988), p. 485.

16. Britain.

17. Britain.

18. Quoted in *The Military Quotation Book* (New York: St. Martin's Press, 1990), p. 39.

19. Fourteen percent say "No," 7 percent say "It depends," and 2 percent say "Don't know." The question, asked as part of a poll of attitudes regarding World War II, was conducted in 1989, before the war in the Persian Gulf.

20. Britain.

21. Light beer and import figures are from Lawrence M. Fisher, "Behind All the Bonhomie, the Brewing Industry Gets Tough," *The New York Times,* July 21, 1991, p. 4. Original: Impact Databank.

22. Spirits in absolute alcohol. Japan wine figure includes sake (11.6 liters).

23. Britain.

24. James Patterson and Peter Kim, *The Day America Told the Truth* (New York: Prentice-Hall, 1991), p. 94.

25. Britain.

26. All figures in this entry from Donald McFarlane, ed., *The Guinness Book of World Records 1991* (New York: Bantam, 1991), p. 570.

27. Salary, winnings, endorsements, and other income included.

28. The three games a week figure was reported in "Harper's Index," *Harper's Magazine,* November 1988, p. 14. A spokesman for the Vice President denied this statistic, while noting that Vice President Quayle plays an average of twice a month, except on vacations when he plays frequently.

READING, WRITING, AND IGNORANCE: EDUCATION AND ACHIEVEMENT

1. The National Commission on Excellence in Education, *A Nation At Risk: The Imperative for Educational Reform* (Washington, D.C.: USGPO, 1983), p. 5.

2. U.S. Bureau of the Census, *Statistical Abstract of the United States 1991* (Washington, D.C.: USGPO, 1991), p. 156. Data for those age 14 to 24.

3. While some American students "may go back for their diplomas, this riddled educational path delays economic returns to the individual and society," says the Council on Competitiveness, "Human Resources," August 1990.

4. Allen Menlo and Pam Poppleton, "A Five-Country Study of the Work Perceptions of Secondary School Teachers in England, the United States, Japan, Singapore and West Germany (1986–1988)," *Comparative Education*, vol. 26, nos. 2/3, 1990.

5. Laubach Literacy International (Syracuse, N.Y.), personal communication. While illiteracy is commonly thought of as the inability to read and perhaps write, *functional* illiteracy is a more important concept. It is "the lack of listening, speaking, reading, writing, and mathematics skills necessary," says Laubach, "to solve the problems one encounters in daily life; to take full advantage of opportunities in one's environment; and to participate fully in the transformation of one's society."

6. A number of developing nations, including Libya and Algeria, spend 9 or 10 percent of their GNP on education. In part, these nations spend so much because they tend to have large school-age populations and relatively small economies. Still, it is worth noting that these countries spend more than the United States and other industrialized nations on education in relative terms. Source: *The Economist Book of Vital World Statistics* (New York: Times Books, 1990), p. 207.

7. National Center for Education Statistics, *Digest of Education Statistics 1991* (Washington, D.C.: U.S. Department of Education, 1991), p. 11. Private spending also includes tuition for many public institutions of higher education.

8. Albert Shanker, "An Oft-told Tale Debunked," in the American Federation of Teachers weekly paid column, *The New York Times,* September 1, 1991, p. E7.

9. New York and New Jersey figures from Jonathan Kozol, *Savage Inequalities* (New York: Crown, 1991), pp. 236–37. New York figures are for the 1989–90 school year, originally from "Statistical Profiles of School Districts" (New York State Board of Education) and *The New York Times.* New Jersey figures are for the 1988–89 school year, originally provided by the Educational Law Center, Newark, N.J. Texas figures are from Children's Defense Fund, *The State of America's Children 1991* (Washington, D.C.: CDF, 1991), p. 84.

10. Public spending can be on public or private schools. Private spending is primarily on private schools, with the exception of tuition at public colleges and universities. Both include current and capital (long-term) expenditures. Also: Ireland, Japan, Italy, and the U.S. are 1986.

11. Spending by ministries of education only.

12. Total spending in 1990 was 7.2 percent of GNP according to National Center for Education Statistics, *Digest of Education Statistics 1991* (Washington, D.C.: U.S. Department of Education, 1991), p. 33. However, since public and

private spending as a percent of GDP are not distinguished, the OECD figure is used in the text.

13. United Nations Development Programme, *Human Development Report 1991* (New York: Oxford University Press, 1991), p. 174.

14. Business leaders in the same survey rate America's "in-company" (or on-the-job) training programs nearly as poorly; we received the sixteenth highest rating of the nineteen major industrial nations, while Japan again was first. Source: *World Competitiveness Report 1991*, published by IMD International, Lausanne, Switzerland, and World Economic Forum, Geneva, Switzerland, p. 339.

15. Survey rating includes Luxembourg.

16. Children's Defense Fund, *The State of America's Children, 1991* (Washington, D.C.: CDF, 1991), p. 6.

17. Ibid., pp. 44–45.

18. U.S. figure is 1990 from National Center for Education Statistics, *Digest of Education Statistics 1991* (Washington, D.C.: U.S. Department of Education, 1991), p. 59. Other figures are 1987–88 from OECD source in text, except Ireland and New Zealand, 1986–87. The figure reported by the OECD for France in 1987–88 is actually 101.7, representing a gross enrollment where students of other ages are grouped with four-year-olds. The OECD's most recent U.S. figure (1986–87) is 49.0 percent.

19. Sam Allis, "Why 180 Days Aren't Enough," *Time,* September 2, 1991, p. 64.

20. School board member Dwight McKenna, who initiated the 220-day program at two elementary schools in New Orleans, is quoted in Sam Allis, "Why 180 Days Aren't Enough," *Time,* September 2, 1991, p. 64.

21. For United Kingdom, England and Wales only; Scotland, 200 days. For Canada, average of two figures, Ontario (186 days) and British Columbia (195 days). For Belgium, average of two figures, Flemish Belgium (160 days) and French Belgium (175 days).

22. Comparisons of higher education sometimes rely on *gross* enrollment figures, whereas the 18.5 percent figure provided in the chart portrays *net* enrollment. *Gross* enrollment ratios measure enrolled students of all ages as a percentage of those in the relevant age group (in this case, age 20 to 24); *net* enrollment measures the percentage of students in the relevant age group who are enrolled. In *gross* enrollment, the U.S. leads with a ratio of 68.1 for 1988, compared to 62.2 for Canada, 34.5 for France, 31.8 for Germany, and 30.1 for Japan. Source: National Center for Education Statistics, *Digest of Education Statistics 1991* (Washington, D.C.: U.S. Department of Education, 1991), pp. 396–97.

23. The G.I. bill allowed many returned servicemen to attend college almost free of charge; during the 1960s, open admissions policies were adopted at

many postsecondary institutions to attract minorities who had previously been shut out of American higher education.

24. Albert Shanker, "An Oft-told Tale Debunked," in the American Federation of Teachers weekly paid column, *The New York Times,* September 1, 1991, p. E7.

25. Denise M. Topolnicki, "Why We Still Live Best," *Money,* October 1991, p. 90.

26. Post-secondary attendance figures are *gross* enrollment figures. See note 22. Qualification figures: Organization for Economic Cooperation and Development, *Education in OECD Countries 1987–88* (Paris: OECD, 1990), p. 112.

27. Richard D. Lamm, "Crisis: The Uncompetitive Society," in Martin K. Starr, ed., *Global Competitiveness* (New York: Norton, 1988), p. 25.

28. National Center for Education Statistics, *Digest of Education Statistics 1991* (Washington, D.C.: U.S. Department of Education, 1991), pp. 22, 169, provides figures that show the rate of full-time higher education enrollment to be 18.5 percent for 1990 among those age 20 to 24 (using 1989 population figures). The UNDP figure is 17.8 percent.

29. Teacher figure: American Federation of Teachers. Others: U.S. Bureau of the Census, *Statistical Abstract of the United States 1991* (Washington, D.C.: USGPO, 1991), p. 146. Salary figures are for 1990.

30. Salary calculations are generally for secondary school teachers. Figures generally include bonuses and supplements. In cases where two figures were provided, lower numbers are used for starting salaries and higher numbers are used for maximum salaries. Also, in the U.S. the maximum teacher pay is reached in about sixteen years; the length of time is less in Australia, Canada, and the United Kingdom, and longer (as much as thirty years) in Japan and Germany. The Canadian figure provided is for Ottawa, Ontario, only. Figures for Saskatchewan are: maximum, 1.91; starting, 1.04. United Kingdom is England and Wales only. Australia is Victoria only. Source: American Federation of Teachers.

31. The Gallup Organization, "Geography: An International Gallup Survey" (Princeton, N.J.: Gallup, 1988), p. 65.

32. Educational Testing Service, *A World of Differences: An International Assessment of Mathematics and Science* (Princeton, N.J.: ETS, 1989), p. 25.

33. The study finds the United States twelfth out of eighteen nations in a test of eighth grade knowledge of math. Among the nineteen major industrial nations included in the IEA study, only Sweden turns in a lower score than the U.S. Japan is first. Source: National Center for Education Statistics, *Digest of Education Statistics 1991* (Washington, D.C.: U.S. Department of Education, 1991), p. 398. Data based on the "Second International Mathematics Study," 1981–82, by the International Association for the Evaluation of Educational Achievement.

34. Canada's figure is an average of seven scores from four provinces: British Columbia, Quebec, Ontario, and New Brunswick. All seven scores are individually higher than the U.S. score.

35. "National Goals for Education," U.S. Department of Education, Washington, D.C., July 1990, p. 6.

36. Karen De Witt, "Math Survey in Public Schools Shows No State Is 'Cutting It,' " *The New York Times,* June 7, 1991, p. A1.

37. Percentage of students who agree with the statement "Much of what you learn in science class is useful in everyday life." Korean students lead the six nations surveyed with 82 percent saying science is useful. Source: Educational Testing Service, *A World of Differences: An International Assessment of Mathematics and Science* (Princeton, N.J.: ETS, 1989), p. 47.

38. The following experiment activities are reported as "high frequency": Watch the teacher do experiments, 19 percent; Do experiments with other students, 16 percent; Do experiments by yourself, 12 percent. The U.S. is comparatively low in all three areas, and last overall when Canada's figures are averaged. Source: Educational Testing Service, *A World of Differences: An International Assessment of Mathematics and Science* (Princeton, N.J.: ETS, 1989), p. 42.

39. English speaking areas only.

40. England.

41. Between 1901 and 1989, the U.S. won 156 Nobel prizes in sciences, compared to 69 in the U.K., 57 in the former West Germany, and just 4 in Japan. Source: U.S. Bureau of the Census, *Statistical Abstract of the United States 1991* (Washington, D.C.: USGPO, 1991), p. 597.

42. Technicians are defined as "persons engaged in scientific research and development activities who have received vocational or technical training for at least three years after the first stage of second-level education." Source: United Nations Development Programme, *Human Development Report 1991* (New York: Oxford University Press, 1991), p. 196.

43. Ibid., p. 174.

44. U.S. science student figures: National Center for Education Statistics, *Digest of Educational Statistics 1991* (Washington, D.C.: U.S. Department of Education, 1991), pp. 274–82; other countries: United Nations Development Programme, *Human Development Report 1991* (New York: Oxford University Press, 1991), pp. 128–89, 174.

45. Another 27 percent say the ability to read a map is "important but not absolutely necessary," and 4 percent say it is "not too important." Source: The Gallup Organization, "Geography: An International Gallup Survey" (Princeton, N.J.: Gallup, 1988), p. 69.

46. Ibid., p. 49.

47. Canada's figures are averages of seven numbers from four provinces: British Columbia, New Brunswick, Ontario, and Quebec. Individually, stu-

dents in all four provinces watch TV less and are less delinquent about home-work than are those in the U.S.

DEBT ON ARRIVAL: THE ECONOMY

1. U.S. Bureau of the Census, *Statistical Abstract of the United States, 1991* (Washington, D.C.: USGPO, 1991), p. 462.

2. For example, Japan and Belgium lead the industrial nations in income held by the poorest 40 percent of the population (22 percent).

3. Figures are after taxes and government transfers. U.S. poverty figures from 1989 are 19.0 percent for children, 11.4 percent for elderly, from the U.S. Bureau of the Census, *Statistical Abstract of the United States 1991* (Washington, D.C.: USGPO, 1991), pp. 462–63. These figures do not reflect government transfers. Original country research for the Luxembourg Income Study database was conducted between 1979 and 1982.

4. Unified Germany (data from former West and East Germany included).

5. *Forbes* press release, July 7, 1991.

6. Gross national product (GNP) is the monetary outcome of goods and services produced by residents of a nation, including income from abroad. Gross domestic product (GDP) is the same as GNP, except it *includes* the output of noncitizens inhabiting a nation and *excludes* residents' foreign income. When comparisons of *GNP per capita* are made among countries, official exchange rates are used to convert national currencies to U.S. dollars. GNP per capita compares actual wealth, but ignores the varying costs of items throughout the world. *Real GDP per capita,* a comparative indicator of wealth developed by the United Nations, is more accurate because it uses purchasing power parities (PPPs), which consider the relative cost of buying the same bundle of items in different countries. Essentially, this means that while the U.S. is sixth in income generated per person, Americans can buy more with their money than can citizens of other nations. In other words, we're the richest.

7. Switzerland, GDP per capita: OECD, personal communication.

8. Denise M. Topolnicki, "Why We Still Live Best," *Money,* October 1991. According to the article, the U.S. home ownership rate is 64 percent; Finland and Australia lead with 69 percent, while Switzerland has the lowest home ownership (30 percent) among the sixteen of the nineteen major industrial nations for which data is available. Original: 1991 Britannica World Data.

9. Rooms counted in a house traditionally include bedrooms, living room, dining room, kitchen, and other major rooms. Foyers, halls, bathrooms, ante-chambers, etc., are not included. All U.S. housing statistics from source in text.

10. The U.S. Department of Housing and Urban Development relies on Martha R. Burt and Barbara E. Cohen, *America's Homeless* (Washington, D.C.: Urban Institute, 1989).

11. The U.S. Department of Housing and Urban Development put the

figure at 250,000–300,000 in 1983, but now uses the Urban Institute's estimate of 500,000–600,000.

12. Canada figure is from the National Anti-Poverty Organization (Ottawa, Canada). This homeless figure, as well as those provided by the U.S. Coalition for the Homeless and the European Federation of National Organizations Working with the Homeless, may include squatters and people living in overcrowded or otherwise insufficient housing arrangements.

13. The United States Conference of Mayors, "A Status Report on Hunger and Homelessness in America's Cities: 1990" (Washington, D.C.: The U.S. Conference of Mayors, 1990), p. 2.

14. U.S. Bureau of the Census, *Statistical Abstract of the United States 1991* (Washington, D.C.: USGPO, 1991), pp. 15–17.

15. Prince Montecuccoli, quoted in *The Military Quotation Book* (New York: St. Martin's Press, 1990), p. 101.

16. George Gallup, Jr., *The Gallup Poll: Public Opinion 1990* (Wilmington, Del.: Scholarly Resources, 1991), p. 5.

17. The International Institute for Strategic Studies, *The Military Balance 1990–1991* (London: Brassey's, 1990), p. 12.

18. Switzerland, 1984; Japan, fiscal year 1989, from Ministry of Finance data provided by the Japanese Consulate (New York City).

19. R&D spending of nations with 0.0 percent is so small that it does not register.

20. Includes Luxembourg.

21. Less of our GNP goes to official development aid than all the nineteen major industrial nations except Spain (.07 percent), which is excluded because it is not a member of the OECD Development Assistance Committee (DAC). The remaining eighteen countries are members of DAC.

22. While the Saudi arms deal has been correctly characterized as a quid pro quo for their cooperation with the U.S. during the Persian Gulf war, $6.1 billion of the $14.5 billion deal was agreed upon before the Iraqi invasion of Kuwait on August 2, 1990. Source: Richard F. Grimmett, "Conventional Arms Transfers to the Third World, 1983–1990," August 2, 1991, a Congressional Research Service report to Congress.

23. This figure includes all French territories. For France alone, $5.16 billion. Source: OECD.

24. Contributions are for 1989, from the Organization for Economic Cooperation and Development.

25. Russell J. Dalton, *Citizen Politics in Western Democracies* (Chatham, N.J.: Chatham House, 1988), p. 103; The Harris Poll, April 8, 1990.

26. This figure includes all French territories. The percentage of GNP for France alone is .54.

27. Gross domestic investment is defined by the World Bank as "outlays on additions to the fixed assets of the economy plus net changes in the level of

inventories." In other words, what Americans invest at home. Gross domestic savings are simpler: GDP minus total consumption. (We also are last in net savings; between 1973 and 1988, our net savings rate was 4.7 percent compared to Japan's 18.7 percent. Source: OECD.)

28. Council on Competitiveness, "Fiscal Policy," January 1990.

29. Figures for 1979 are from the Organization for Economic Cooperation and Development, *OECD Economic Outlook 50* (Paris: OECD, 1991), p. 203.

30. American Financial Services Association press release, March 6, 1991.

31. Heron House, *The Book of Numbers* (New York: A&W Publishers, 1978), pp. 422–23.

32. John Allen Paulos, *Innumeracy* (New York: Vintage, 1990), p. 3.

33. Educational Testing Service, *A World of Differences: An International Assessment of Mathematics and Science* (Princeton, N.J.: ETS, 1989), p. 24.

34. Includes Social Security trusts (on-line budget deficit, therefore, is $331 billion in 1991, $425 billion in 1992). Source: Congressional Budget Office, *The Economic and Budget Outlook: An Update,* August, 1991.

35. Debt figures are for 1989 from the *World Competitiveness Report 1991,* published by IMD International, Lausanne, Switzerland, and World Economic Forum, Geneva, Switzerland, p. 249.

36. Denmark, Ireland, and Spain are 1987. U.S. figures are 1991, percent of GNP, from CBO source in text. Other figures are 1989; U.S. deficit figure for 1989 is $144 billion (2.8 percent of GDP). Projections for 1991 from *OECD Economic Outlook 50* (Paris: OECD, 1991) are bleaker for the U.K., Germany, and Canada.

37. James Sterngold, "Intractable Trade Issues With Japan," *The New York Times,* December 4, 1991, p. D4. Sources for all other trade data in this section: The World Bank, *World Development Report 1991* (New York: Oxford University Press, 1991), p. 231, Council on Competitiveness, "Trade," May 1990; U.S. Department of Commerce, *U.S. Foreign Trade Highlights 1990,* April 1991; International Monetary Fund, *Direction of Trade Statistics Yearbook 1990* (Washington, D.C.: IMF, 1990).

38. World Health Organization, *World Health Statistics Annual, 1990* (Geneva: WHO, 1991), p. 30.

39. David Sanger, "As Ugly Feelings Grow, It's Hard to Separate Fact and Fiction," *The New York Times,* January 26, 1992, section 4, p. 1; Steven R. Weisman, "A Deep Split In Attitudes Is Developing," *The New York Times,* December 3, 1991, p. A16.

40. Companies are ranked by size of sales.

41. The American banks include Citicorp, Chase Manhattan, BankAmerica, J. P. Morgan, Security Pacific, Chemical, Manufacturers Hanover, Bankers Trust, and First Chicago. In August 1991, Chemical Bank and Manufacturers Hanover announced they would merge, a further indicator of their financial troubles.

42. Source: Congressional Budget Office, *The Economic and Budget Outlook: An Update,* August, 1991.

43. The Federal Reserve Bank notes: "These measures may actually understate the performance of German and Swiss banks, since unreported earnings and hidden reserves at these institutions tend to conceal additional underlying strength in profitability . . ." Regardless, the U.S. still performs the worst.

44. While our industrial productivity is declining and Japan's and Germany's are increasing, the U.S. still has the highest rate of industrial productivity (largest GDP per worker).

45. Figures for Austria and Ireland are 1988. Figure for Denmark is 1986.

46. International Labor Organization, *Yearbook of Labor Statistics 1989–90* (Geneva: ILO, 1990), pp. 687–92.

47. Includes Luxembourg.

48. James E. Heard, president of Institutional Shareholder Services, quoted in: Steve Lohr, "Recession Puts a Harsh Spotlight on Hefty Pay of Top Executives," *The New York Times,* January 20, 1992, p. A1. Salary figures for executives in top thirty companies from same source. Original: Graef S. Crystal, University of California at Berkeley.

49. Remuneration includes salary, benefits, perquisites, and long-term incentives, before taxes, for chief executive officers (CEOs) in organizations with sales of $250 million or more. Remuneration for manufacturing employees includes basic compensation and company contributions.

50. Figures were provided for major (usually capital) cities in each country and therefore may not reflect trends in nonurban areas. For countries where more than one city was included (e.g., Dusseldorf and Frankfurt; Chicago, Houston, Los Angeles, and New York), figures were averaged. Incidentally, all four U.S. cities reported fewer vacation days than the next lowest country on the list, Canada.

DEMOCRACY'S BUREAUCRACIES: POLITICS

1. E. J. Dionne, *Why Americans Hate Politics* (New York: Simon & Schuster, 1991), p. 10.

2. $3 million per candidate and $6 million to unopposed candidates: figures from Richard D. Lamm, "Crisis: The Uncompetitive Society," in Martin K. Starr, ed., *Global Competitiveness* (New York: Norton, 1988), p. 31; $160 million figure from Larry Makinson, "PACs in Profile: Industry & Interest Spending in the 1990 Elections" (Washington, D.C.: Center for Responsive Politics, 1991); quote from Common Cause president Fred Wertheimer, *Facts on File,* vol. 50, no. 2582, May 18, 1990, p. 359.

3. George Gallup, Jr., *The Gallup Poll: Public Opinion 1990* (Wilmington, Del.: Scholarly Resources, 1991), p. 140.

4. Ibid., p. 178. Emphasis added.

5. P. J. O'Rourke, *Parliament of Whores* (New York: Atlantic Monthly Press, 1991).

6. Switzerland's voting rate is lower (44 percent), though they aren't comparable because their quasi-independent cantons make them more of a confederation than a single state, especially when it comes to voting nationally. Also, only 36 percent of eligible Americans voted in 1990 congressional elections. Source: Committee for the Study of the American Electorate, in *Facts on File*, vol. 50, no. 2607, November 9, 1990, p. 832.

7. U.S. Bureau of the Census, *Statistical Abstract of the United States 1991* (Washington, D.C.: USGPO, 1991), p. 268.

8. 57.4 percent said they voted in 1988, but only 50.1 actually cast votes, according to the U.S. Bureau of the Census, *Statistical Abstract of the United States 1991* (Washington, D.C.: USGPO, 1991), pp. 268–70.

9. For the U.S., the turnout rate is from the 1988 presidential election: U.S. Bureau of the Census, *Statistical Abstract of the United States 1991* (Washington, D.C.: USGPO, 1991), p. 270. Spain's figure is from G. Bingham Powell, "American Voter Turnout in Comparative Perspective," *American Political Science Review*, vol. 80, no. 1, March 1986. For the remainder of the countries, the rate is an average turnout from 1971–80, the most recent years for which data is available.

10. Britain (for voter interest).

11. Britain.

12. Includes Luxembourg.

13. Russell J. Dalton, *Citizen Politics in Western Democracies* (Chatham, N.J.: Chatham House, 1988), p. 108.

14. U.S. figure is 1991 median usual weekly earnings of full-time wage and salary workers, from the U.S. Bureau of Labor Statistics. Other figures are 1986–1989 from the other sources mentioned in the text. Comparisons are of hourly, weekly, or monthly wages in nonagricultural activities generally.

15. Switzerland is not a member of the U.N.

16. Includes regular budget contributions only. The U.S. leads in outstanding contributions to peacekeeping operations as well—$140.9 million as of December 31, 1991.

17. Multiple-nation vetoes are not unusual. All of France's vetoes since 1980 have been with the U.K. and the U.S.; all of the U.K.'s vetoes since 1980 have been with the U.S. and/or France; and fifteen of the U.S.'s vetoes since 1980 have been with the U.K. and/or France.

18. The ICCPR and ICESCR were approved by the General Assembly in 1966 and went into effect in 1976. The U.S. signed both in 1977, but has yet to ratify either. The U.N. Convention against Torture was approved by the General Assembly in 1984 and went into effect in 1987. The U.S. signed in 1988 and ratified in 1990. Source: Amnesty International, personal communication.

19. Switzerland also has ratified only one of the treaties, though it is not a member of the U.N. and should not, therefore, be subject to the same standard.

20. *Amnesty International Report 1991* (New York: Amnesty International, 1991), p. 273.

21. Personal communication.

22. New Zealand and Sweden also ratified the Optional Protocol to ICCPR and the Second Optional Protocol to ICCPR Aiming at the Abolition of the Death Penalty. Austria, Canada, Denmark, Finland, France, Ireland, Italy, the Netherlands, Norway, and Spain also ratified the former; Australia ratified the latter.

TRIALS AND TRIBULATIONS: CRIME AND THE LEGAL SYSTEM

1. U.S. Department of Justice, *Sourcebook of Criminal Justice Statistics 1990* (Washington, D.C.: USGPO, 1991), p. 177.

2. George Gallup, Jr., *The Gallup Poll: Public Opinion 1990* (Wilmington, Del.: Scholarly Resources, 1991), p. 123. "Harsher punishment" was the leading answer (not including "other").

3. Marc Mauer, "Americans Behind Bars: A Comparison of International Rates of Incarceration" (Washington, D.C.: The Sentencing Project, 1991), p. 7.

4. England and Wales only. Scotland, 18.6 percent. Northern Ireland, 15.0 percent.

5. Japanese inhabitants, twenty years of age and older, were polled face-to-face, while respondents in other nations were generally polled by phone.

6. Ranking God's importance: World Values Survey; average U.S. number from Russell J. Dalton, *Citizen Politics in Western Democracies* (Chatham, N.J.: Chatham House, 1988), p. 111.

7. World Values Survey: 94.6 percent of Americans say that "Thou shalt not kill" applies fully, 4.2 percent say it applies "to a limited extent." Only 1.2 percent—or 12 out of 1,000 people surveyed—say it does not apply.

8. John McCormick and Bill Turque, "Big Crimes, Small Cities," *Newsweek,* June 10, 1991, p. 16.

9. U.S. figure is 1990 from U.S. Department of Justice, *Uniform Crime Reports 1990* (Washington, D.C.: USGPO, 1991), p. 8. Statistics from Interpol (the International Criminal Police Organization) are based on crimes reported to or detected by police and may be somewhat incomparable or incomplete. They are, however, the most reliable international figures available.

10. Henry Wadsworth Longfellow, *Hyperion* (1839), quoted in Gorton Carruth and Eugene Ehrlich, *The Harper Book of American Quotations* (New York: Harper & Row, 1988), p. 634.

11. Violent deaths are categorized as those caused by homicide, suicide, or motor vehicle accidents. Young adults here refers to those age 15 to 24 (see

the U.S. House of Representatives Select Committee on Children, Youth, and Families' March 1990 report, "Children's Well-Being: An International Comparison" [Washington, D.C.: USGPO, 1990], p. 54).

12. U.K. figure is England and Wales only; Canada figure is from: Bret C. Williams and Jonathan B. Kotch, "Excess Injury Mortality in the United States: Comparison of Recent International Statistics," *Pediatrics,* vol. 86, no. 6, December 1990, p. 1071.

13. U.S. Department of Justice, *Uniform Crime Reports 1990* (Washington, D.C.: USGPO, 1991), p. 12.

14. George Gallup, Jr., *The Gallup Poll: Public Opinion 1990* (Wilmington, Del.: Scholarly Resources, 1991), p. 124. The bill had not been acted upon by President Bush at the time of publication.

15. China, Iran, and South Africa may execute more criminals than the U.S., but other democratic nations have essentially discontinued capital punishment. Japan, the only one of the nineteen major industrial nations besides the U.S. that still uses the death penalty, has executed fifteen people in the last decade, one fifth as many as the U.S. per capita. Source: Amnesty International.

16. Capital punishment was much more common in the early part of the century; between 1930 and 1939, 1,667 Americans were executed under civil authority, including 125 for rape; U.S. Bureau of the Census, *Statistical Abstract of the United States 1991* (Washington, D.C.: USGPO, 1991), p. 197.

17. Ibid., p. 196.

18. U.S. Department of Justice, *Sourcebook of Criminal Justice Statistics 1990* (Washington, D.C.: USGPO, 1991), p. 201.

19. James Patterson and Peter Kim, *The Day America Told the Truth* (New York: Prentice-Hall, 1991), p. 237.

20. Death Penalty Information Center press release.

21. 1985.

22. Mary P. Koss, University of Arizona, College of Medicine, personal communication.

23. U.S. Bureau of the Census, *Statistical Abstract of the United States 1991* (Washington, D.C.: USGPO, 1991), p. 181.

24. Mary P. Koss, W. J. Woodruff, and Paul G. Koss, "Criminal Victimization among Primary Care Medical Patients: Prevalence, Incidence, and Physician Usage," *Behavioral Sciences and the Law,* 9(1991):85–96.

25. Percentage who said they were raped "or forced to have sex against their will." Fewer black young women say they were raped. Two percent of white men and 6 percent of black men say they were raped at age 20 or younger. Source: Kristin Anderson Moore, Christine Winquist Nord, and James L. Peterson, "Nonvoluntary Sexual Activity Among Adolescents," *Family Planning Perspectives,* 20 (May–June 1989): 110–14.

26. 12.8 percent for the U.S. vs. 9.9 percent for most industrial nations,

according to Jan J. M. van Dijk et al., *Experiences of Crime across the World* (Boston: Kluwer, 1991), p. 177.

27. U.S. Department of Justice, *Sourcebook of Criminal Justice Statistics 1990* (Washington, D.C.: USGPO, 1991), p. 153.

28. George Gallup, Jr., *The Gallup Poll: Public Opinion 1990* (Wilmington, Del.: Scholarly Resources, 1991), p. 123.

29. U.S. Department of Justice, *Sourcebook of Criminal Justice Statistics 1990* (Washington, D.C.: USGPO, 1991), pp. 595, 647.

30. United Nations, *Report of the International Narcotics Control Board for 1990* (New York: United Nations, 1990), p. 31.

31. Portugal also seizes more cocaine per capita.

32. For Belgium, Denmark, and Ireland figures represent number of drug *offenses* known to police. The number of offenders is probably somewhat lower, therefore, as many offenders commit multiple offenses.

33. Austria's cocaine figure, 1981. Also, cocaine is classified here as base and salts, as opposed to coca leaf. Marijuana is cannabis herb, not plants or resin.

34. Figures of 0.0 for Norway, Ireland, and Japan are due to rounding; each country had less than 0.05 kilos of cocaine seized per 1,000,000 inhabitants.

35. Five states (California, Vermont, Utah, Oregon, and Maine) have adopted .08 percent limits, according to MADD.

36. U.S. figure is 1990 from Mothers Against Drunk Driving (MADD). Other figures are 1983 from M. Adrian et al., except the Netherlands, Sweden, Spain, and Yugoslavia, which are 1982.

37. Denise M. Topolnicki, "Why We Still Live Best," *Money,* October 1991, p. 91.

38. Britain.

39. George Gallup, Jr., *The Gallup Poll: Public Opinion 1990* (Wilmington, Del.: Scholarly Resources, 1991), p. 125; additional Gallup poll information provided by Handgun Control, Inc. (Washington, D.C.).

40. For gun ownership: England and Wales. Percentage gun ownership in Scotland: 0.4. In Northern Ireland: 1.6. For percentage saying self-defense killing can be justified: Britain.

41. Quoted in Richard W. Moll, *The Lure of the Law* (New York: Penguin, 1990), p. 4.

42. Press release of the Vice-President's office, August 13, 1991.

43. Author's interview with Marc Galanter, Director, Institute for Legal Studies, University of Wisconsin—Madison Law School.

44. The President's Council on Competitiveness, "Agenda for Civil Justice Reform In America" (August, 1991), p. 1: "A recent article in *Forbes* estimates that individuals, businesses and government spend more than $80 billion a year on direct litigation costs and higher insurance premiums, and a total of up to $300 billion indirectly, including the costs of efforts to avoid liability." The American Bar Association takes issue with these figures, presented by Vice-

President Quayle, saying that the majority of the 18 million cases filed annually are divorce and small claims cases. In addition, they question the validity of the $80 billion and $300 billion figures. See: Talbot S. D'Alemberte, "ABA's Retort to Quayle is No Joke," letter to the editor, *The Wall Street Journal,* September 18, 1991, p. A15.

45. Walter K. Olson, *The Litigation Explosion* (New York: Truman Talley, 1991), p. 2.

46. Quoted in Richard W. Moll, *The Lure of the Law* (New York: Penguin, 1990), p. 4.

47. Myron Moskovitz, quoted in ibid., p. 10.

48. United Kingdom includes barristers and solicitors, including some solicitors without practicing certificates. Some figures are rounded estimates.

49. As specified in the text, the number of lawyers per 100,000 is 13 but the number of professionals who perform tasks carried out by lawyers in other nations (i.e., lawyers and lawyer equivalents) is 93 per 100,000, according to a letter from an attorney familiar with the Japanese legal system, *The New York Times,* August 23, 1991, p. A26.

50. Walter K. Olson, *The Litigation Explosion* (New York: Truman Talley, 1991), p. 18.

51. World Values Survey.

52. U.S. Department of Justice, *Sourcebook of Criminal Justice Statistics 1990* (Washington, D.C.: USGPO, 1991), p. 191.

53. Britain.

GLUTTONS GALORE: THE ENVIRONMENT, ENERGY, AND TRANSPORTATION

1. Louis Harris and Associates, *Public and Leadership Attitudes to the Environment in Four Continents: A Report of a Survey in 16 Countries* (New York: Louis Harris, 1989), pp. 33, 161; Survey Research Consultants International, *Index to International Public Opinion 1988–89* (New York: Greenwood Press, 1990), p. 653.

2. Rose Gutfeld, "Eight of 10 Americans Are Environmentalists, At Least So They Say," *The Wall Street Journal,* August 2, 1991, p. 1.

3. World Resources Institute, *World Resources 1990–91* (New York: Oxford University Press, 1990), p. 345.

4. Ibid., p. 25.

5. Includes "fossil fuel combustion and flaring of natural gas," while excluding cement production and deforestation (Organization for Economic Cooperation and Development, *Environmental Indicators* [Paris: OECD, 1991], pp. 16, 68). The latter two factors are included in carbon emissions in the previous greenhouse gas emissions chart provided by the World Resources Institute.

6. Organization for Economic Cooperation and Development, *The State of the Environment* (Paris: OECD, 1991), p. 47.

7. Canada releases more sulfur oxides per capita. Source: Organization for Economic Cooperation and Development, *Environmental Indicators* (Paris: OECD, 1991), p. 21.

8. Sources: U.S.: Organization for Economic Cooperation and Development, *Environmental Indicators* (Paris: OECD, 1991), p. 21; China: World Resources Institute, *World Resources 1990–91* (New York: Oxford University Press, 1990), p. 352.

9. Organization for Economic Cooperation and Development, *The State of the Environment* (Paris: OECD, 1991), p. 47.

10. Ibid., p. 49. The major industrial nations referred to here are OECD nations.

11. Ibid., p. 255. Specific numbers are provided in the source, but they are not fully comparable.

12. Ruth Leger Sivard, *World Military and Social Expenditures 1989* (Washington, D.C.: World Priorities, 1989), p. 50. A figure of 100 percent is reported for the U.S.

13. Ibid., p. 52. The Cambodia figure is also reported in: United Nations Development Programme, *Human Development Report 1990* (New York: Oxford University Press, 1990), p. 130.

14. Alan Durning, "Asking How Much is Enough," in Lester R. Brown et al., *State of the World 1991* (New York: Norton, 1991), p. 160.

15. Figures for Japan include noncarbonated drinks. German figures include the former West and East Germany. U.K. figures are from Britain only.

16. Organization for Economic Cooperation and Development, *The State of the Environment* (Paris: OECD, 1991), p. 54.

17. Australia, 1975; Ireland, 1972.

18. World Resources Institute, *World Resources 1990–91* (New York: Oxford University Press, 1990), p. 42.

19. John W. Wright, ed., *The Universal Almanac 1991* (Kansas City, Mo.: Andrews and McMeel, 1990), p. 319.

20. World Resources Institute, *World Resources 1990–91* (New York: Oxford University Press, 1990), p. 294.

21. Organization for Economic Cooperation and Development, *The State of the Environment* (Paris: OECD, 1991), p. 114.

22. Organization for Economic Cooperation and Development, *Environmental Indicators* (Paris: OECD, 1991), p. 45.

23. Organization for Economic Cooperation and Development, *Environmental Indicators* (Paris: OECD, 1991), p. 47.

24. Canada's figure is an estimate; where two figures were available, the higher number has been used.

25. New Zealand's figure includes reusable bottles; Canada's figure is an estimate. According to the United States Environmental Protection Agency's 1988 figures (released in 1990), 12 percent of our glass is recycled. In addition,

only 5.8 percent of metals, 2.3 percent of rubber and leather, and 1.1 percent of plastics are recycled.

26. Organization for Economic Cooperation and Development, *The State of the Environment* (Paris: OECD, 1991), p. 152.

27. Ibid., p. 145.

28. Ibid., p. 152.

29. Ibid., p. 151.

30. U.S. figures for hazardous waste include "waste waters managed in land-based operations." Source: Organization for Economic Cooperation and Development, *Environmental Indicators* (Paris: OECD, 1991), p. 73. This might explain why the U.S. figures are inordinately greater than the others, yet a spokesperson at the Environmental Defense Fund says the 275 million tons of hazardous waste provided by the OECD is low if it indeed does include waste waters. With waste waters, annual hazardous waste production in the U.S. may be closer to 747 million tons.

31. By law, all industrial waste in Japan is treated. Waste is deemed hazardous only if after the treatment process the substance "exceeds its relevant concentration criterion." Organization for Economic Cooperation and Development, *Environmental Indicators* (Paris: OECD, 1991), p. 73.

32. Figures are as of the end of 1988; World Resources Institute, *World Resources 1990–91* (New York: Oxford University Press, 1990), p. 144.

33. *The Economist Book of Vital World Statistics* (New York: Times Books, 1990), p. 79. The United States generates 173 million tons (coal equivalent) of nuclear energy, compared to 77 million tons in the USSR and 43 million tons in France.

34. World Resources Institute, *World Resources 1990–91* (New York: Oxford University Press, 1990), pp. 143–4.

35. Damage from the Chernobyl accident appears to have been highly underestimated (or even misrepresented) at first. "In March 1989, the Soviet Communist Party newspaper *Pravda* published a report that the contamination was much more extensive than previously acknowledged," says World Resources Institute, *World Resources 1990–91*, p. 157. Before Chernobyl, the Three Mile Island accident in the United States galvanized opposition to nuclear energy.

36. Organization for Economic Cooperation and Development, *The State of the Environment* (Paris: OECD, 1991), p. 228.

37. Represents number of reactors in unified Germany; twenty-three reactors are operable in former West Germany, five are operable in former East Germany according to the source listed in the text. All six of the inoperable reactors are in the former West Germany.

38. Twenty-two of the U.S. tests were conducted jointly between the United Kingdom and the United States.

39. *Autoweek*, September 2, 1991, p. 9. Original: Runzheimer International.

Figures are for self-serve unleaded regular gasoline, except Tokyo, which is full-serve leaded.

40. Compound growth rates, not average annual percentage change, are used for Australia and Canada. As a result, these figures are not directly comparable to the others in the chart. Figures for Belgium include Luxembourg.

41. A major spill is defined as being over 25,000 tons of oil or over $5 million of indemnity.

42. Organization for Economic Cooperation and Development, *The State of the Environment* (Paris: OECD, 1991), p. 214; United Nations, *Compendium of Social Statistics and Indicators 1988* (New York: United Nations, 1991), pp. 544–53.

43. Other options were pedestrian or bicycle travel in all nations listed except the Soviet Union and Poland.

44. Unified Germany; New Zealand, 1982; 1988 figures place U.S. rail travel at half the 1986 number, but they exclude commuter railroad travel.

FAX AT OUR FINGERTIPS: MEDIA, ARTS, AND TECHNOLOGY

1. *The World Almanac and Book of Facts 1992* (New York: Pharos Books, 1991), p. 318. Original: A.C. Nielsen.

2. Data was collected before the 1990 reunification of East and West Germany. It is also important to note that East Germany's newspapers were largely controlled by the government at the time of data collection.

3. Newspaper figures for the United Kingdom, Japan, and the United States are 1986; however, 1990 figures from the American Newspaper Publishers Association show U.S. newspaper circulation per capita to be unchanged. Denmark's radio figure is 1980. For radio and television sets, some figures are estimates while others represent sets licensed or declared.

4. *Information Please Almanac 1992* (Boston: Houghton Mifflin, 1992), p. 737; *The World Almanac and Book of Facts 1992* (New York: Pharos Books, 1991), pp. 317–18.

5. Belgium is an average of two figures: Flanders (15:58) and Wallonia (24:17). Japan is Kansai area only; Kanto area figure is 27:39. Also, Nielsen's figures generally refer to household viewing of television (two or more people).

6. All U.S. VCR figures are from Electronic Industries Association, *The U.S. Consumer Electronics Industry in Review, 1991 Edition* (Washington, D.C.: Electronic Industries Association, 1991), pp. 29–67.

7. UNESCO, *Statistical Yearbook 1990* (Paris: UNESCO, 1990), Table 9.1.

8. United Nations Development Programme, *Human Development Report 1991* (New York: Oxford University Press, 1991), p. 182.

9. U.S. figure is estimated household penetration as of June 1991 from Electronic Industries Association, *The U.S. Consumer Electronics Industry in*

Review, 1991 Edition (Washington, D.C.: Electronic Industries Association, 1991), p. 67. Other figures are 1988–89 from Euromonitor sources in text.

10. Ireland, 1985. Hong Kong and Singapore, 1983. North Korea, 1985. Vietnam, 1984.

11. The former East Germany's figure is 4.2 films attended per year on average.

12. John W. Wright, ed., *The Universal Almanac 1991* (Kansas City, Mo.: Andrews and McMeel, 1990), p. 239. Original: *Publishers Weekly* and *Book Industry Trends.*

13. United Nations Development Programme, *Human Development Report 1991* (New York: Oxford University Press, 1991), p. 185.

14. Philosophy and psychology books are not distinguished by the Library of Congress or *Publishers Weekly,* the most reliable source for numbers of books published in different disciplines annually in the U.S. Therefore, 828 is a high estimate for the number of philosophy books published in the U.S., as it represents half of the 1,656 titles listed under "philosophy/psychology" by *Publishers Weekly* (R. R. Bowker Co., N.Y., 1988, in U.S. Bureau of the Census, *Statistical Abstract of the United States 1990* [Washington, D.C.: USGPO, 1990], p. 227). The number of philosophy books is probably lower; we may publish far fewer new philosophy titles per 1 million population annually than is stated in the text.

15. U.S. figures are 1991, American Association of Museums, personal communication; others are 1984–87 with the exception of Sweden, 1983.

16. U.S. figures for number of museums include those catalogued by the American Association of Museums, including aquariums, art museums, children's museums, general museums, historic houses, history museums, natural history museums, planetariums, science museums, and specialized museums, but excluding arboretums (318), nature centers (297), and zoos (133) because these institutions are not included in international museum tallies.

17. Total expenditure in 1988–89, the same year as the advertising figures in the text above, on higher education was $135.9 billion, in 1989–90, $143.2 billion. Source: National Center for Education Statistics, *Digest of Education Statistics, 1990* (Washington, D.C.: U.S. Department of Education, 1991), p. 33.

18. Advertising expenditures from *Advertising Age,* January 6, 1992, p. 52.

CONCLUSION

1. Richard D. Lamm, "Crisis: The Uncompetitive Society," in Martin K. Starr, ed., *Global Competitiveness* (New York: Norton, 1988), p. 39.

ACKNOWLEDGMENTS

Grateful acknowledgment is made to the following for permission to reprint statistical data:

Educational Testing Service: Statistics from *A World of Difference: An International Assessment of Mathematics and Sciences* are reprinted by permission of Educational Testing Service, the copyright owner.

Forbes Inc.: Statistics from the following issues of *Forbes:* July 23, 1990, July 22, 1991, August 19, 1991, and October 21, 1991, are © Forbes Inc. Reprinted by permission of Forbes Inc.

Ronald Inglehart: Statistics from the *World Values Survey (1981)* are reprinted by permission of Ronald Inglehart of the Institute for Social Research, University of Michigan.

International Labour Office: Statistics from *International Labour Statistics 1989–1990,* pp. 46–119, 120–186, 687–692. Copyright 1990 by International Labour Organisation, Geneva. Statistics from "Work and Family: The Child Care Challenge," *Conditions of Work Digest,* vol. 7, February 1988, p. 20.

The New England Journal of Medicine: Statistics from "Comparisons of National Cesarean-Section Rates," by Francis C. Norton, Paul J. Placek, and Selma M. Taffel, *NEJM,* vol. 316, no. 7, February 12, 1987, p. 387. Reprinted by permission of *The New England Journal of Medicine.*

Pediatrics: Statistics from "Immunization Coverage Among Preschool Children: The United States and Selected European Countries," by Bret C. Williams. Reprinted by permission of *Pediatrics.*

Pergamon Press: Statistics from *Science Achievement in Seventeen Countries, A Preliminary Report,* by the International Association for the Evaluation of Educational Achievement, 1988. Reprinted by permission of Pergamon Press plc, Headington Hill Hall, Headington, Oxford, OX3 OBW.

Times Books: Statistics from *The Economist Book of Vital World Statistics,* by the editors of *The Economist.* Copyright © 1990 by the Economist Books Ltd. Reprinted by permission of Times Books, a Division of Random House, Inc.

Towers Perrin: Statistics from *Worldwide Total Remuneration 1991* and *Tort Cost Trends: An International Perspective.* Reprinted by permission of Towers Perrin.

United Nations Children Fund (UNICEF): Statistics from *The State of the World's Children, 1991.* Reprinted by permission of UNICEF, 3 United Nations Plaza, New York, NY 10017.

World Health Organization: Statistics from *World Health Statistics Annual 1990* (Geneva, 1991). Reprinted by permission of the World Health Organization.

ABOUT THE AUTHOR

Andrew L. Shapiro is a teacher, a writer, and a staff member of *The Nation* magazine. He was graduated from Brown University in 1990 and now lives in New York City.